Presented to

_____

On the occasion of

_____

From

_____

Date

_____

GOD'S WORD FOR
Couples

Toni Sortor and Pamela McQuade

HUMBLECREEK
INSPIRATION FOR LIFE

Published by Humble Creek, P. O. Box 719, Uhrichsville, Ohio 44683

Printed in the United States of America.

5 4 3 2

GOD'S WORD FOR
Couples

INTRODUCTION

God created the institution of marriage. He offers marriage as a blessing to us, but our actual relationships are only what we make of them. When, through conscious effort, we put good things into them, our relationships will improve.

God's Word for Couples is designed to encourage married couples to insert positive elements into their relationships through Bible reading and prayer. Through this book, readers will be challenged to consider how God's Word relates to their lives and to practice His commands.

May this book bless you as you live and love.

Trust God's Faithfulness

Then Isaac sowed in that land,
and received in the same year
*an hundredfold: and the L*ORD *blessed him.*

GENESIS 26:12 KJV

When God told Isaac to take his wife and make his home in Egypt, Isaac obeyed, even though he was afraid for his life. In return for his faithfulness, the Lord blessed Isaac, increasing his investment a hundred times over in one year.

What is God telling you and your spouse this year? Would you rather live somewhere else, do something else, even be someone else? Do you want to argue the point or pretend you didn't get the message, or are you willing to trust God's guidance and faithfulness? On the first day of a new year, take time as a couple to discuss where you think God wants you to be this year and what you hope He will help you accomplish in the next 365 days.

Father, we ask Your guidance for this year, confident that wherever You send us, we will be protected and blessed.

Work as a Team

There is no fear in love,
but perfect love casts out fear.

1 JOHN 4:18 NRSV

Since none of us is going to reach perfection during this lifetime, on occasion we will experience some fear in our relationships. For most, these fears will be minor: spending a little too much for an unnecessary luxury, gaining a little too much weight, making a decision without consulting the other, and so on. Actually, we don't fear our spouses' reactions as much as we wonder what they will think of us. Will they trust us as much as before?

Learning to work as a team and trusting the other member takes time. As the years go by, we become more attuned to our partners. We discover what bugs them and what doesn't, and out of love—not fear—we adjust our actions. In time, there will be no fear between us, only patience and understanding.

Father, help us in this job of removing fear and uncertainty from our relationship. Help us to grow in confidence and love as a couple.

ACCEPTANCE

Did the contempt of families
terrify me, that I kept silence,
and went not out of the door?

JOB 31:34 KJV

L et's face it, not everyone in your family is going to love
your spouse immediately. Most of them will accept your
choice, but one or two may not be much more than civil, con-
sidering her or him "beneath you" for one reason or another.

Avoiding those critical family members because of fear or
anger serves nothing. It is better to show up at family events
and keep on smiling, even if you're seething inside. With
time, your spouse will prove to be "good enough" through the
strength of your marriage, shared family experiences, and any
children you may be blessed with. We cannot demand acceptance from anyone; we have to earn it, one day at a time.

Father, give us the patience we need to become valued members of
our spouse's family. With time, they will realize how good we are
for each other.

PATIENCE AND PERSEVERANCE

"And you have persevered
and have patience, and have labored
for My name's sake and
have not become weary."

REVELATION 2:3 NKJV

M arriage is hard work, especially when it's new. Who would have thought that squeezing the toothpaste in the middle could be the basis of a two-day fight? Or that such a buttoned-down husband would be incapable of putting his dirty shorts in the hamper? How could such a lovely woman go to bed in flannel, even in summer? The list goes on.

If you can get over these little problems, you will have the foundation of a strong marriage. Still, patience and perseverance are required: You need to come to acceptable compromises without becoming weary and, at the same time, keep working on the little issues that drive you crazy.

Lord, we are determined that our marriage is not going to suffer because of petty annoyances. Remind us of this promise when we disagree, and show us how we can overcome our differences.

HOLD HANDS

Can two walk together,
unless they are agreed?

AMOS 3:3 NKJV

How long has it been since the two of you took an old-fashioned walk? Not a power walk, a jog, and certainly not a run, but a leisurely, rambling walk, just for the fun of it.

Granted, the weather may not be perfect for walking, but that only means your walk will be more private. If there's a thunderstorm or blizzard raging, head for the nearest mall, with no shopping allowed.

Remember, not every activity requires a goal, and not all of our leisure time should be productive. What about just getting out of the house to admire God's world and spend some time with the one you love? Hold hands, bump shoulders, giggle a lot, and talk about your hopes and dreams. Just the two of you.

Father, help us realize that being together without purpose can be a
wonderful experience that draws us closer.

Agree to Disagree

But avoid foolish controversies
and genealogies and arguments
and quarrels about the law,
because these are unprofitable and useless.

TITUS 3:9 NIV

B efore falling in love, couples seldom have the time to discuss their stands on all possible "issues." Life simply doesn't work that way. We generally check out the most important qualities for compatibility—religion, political beliefs, personality—and leave the rest for later. This is not necessarily bad because, if you dig deeply enough, you could spend your life looking for the "perfect" spouse.

You're not perfect, after all, and sometimes you and your spouse will disagree. The Book of Titus tells us that some of these disagreements just aren't worth fighting over. When, after a few minutes of discussion, it becomes obvious that neither of you is going to change the other's mind, you both have to back off and agree to disagree.

Lord, we realize that any two people will sometimes disagree. Please teach us to recognize the point at which further discussion becomes "unprofitable and useless" and have the sense to back off.

THE PAST

O God, you know my folly;
the wrongs I have done
are not hidden from you.

PSALM 69:5 NRSV

Exactly how much does your spouse need to know about your past? What should you confess to before and during marriage? Unfortunately, no one has compiled an up-to-date list. Certainly, you must admit to any sin that might put your partner in moral or physical danger, but how "big" must a wrongdoing be to qualify? Even if you decide on total confession of all your past sins, you still have to make judgment calls. What about that crush on your sixth-grade teacher? Or the quarters you lifted from your mother's purse? Or the other person you once thought of marrying?

God knows every wrong you have ever committed, confessed, or hidden. If your conscience is burdened, ask Him for guidance on what you need to reveal. Trust Him to indicate what needs to be shared and what would be better off unsaid.

Father, we all have our little secrets. Help us to identify those we need to share with each other and those that would only hurt our partners.

FRIENDS

Behold, I send you forth as
sheep in the midst of wolves:
be ye therefore wise as serpents,
and harmless as doves.

MATTHEW 10:16 KJV

Not everyone you meet as a couple will have your best interests at heart. Some will pretend to be friends with ulterior motives in mind, some will be cheats and liars, and still others will try to corrupt your relationship. But notice that Jesus did not say to isolate yourselves from the world. You should get out there and live your lives, using wariness, good judgment, and intelligence in your dealings with the world's wolves.

At the same time, you are to remain as harmless as doves, never lowering yourselves to the level of the wolves, and never striking out in retaliation. As a Christian couple, you may become a target, but no one says you have to stand there and wait for the bullet.

Father, our lifestyle is not that of the world, and we may find ourselves in conflict with others because of our faith. When we do, give us the wisdom to avoid being hurt and the strength not to hurt in return.

LEARNING PATIENCE

Wait on the LORD:
be of good courage,
and he shall strengthen thine heart:
wait, I say, on the LORD.

PSALM 27:14 KJV

The idea of patience is not a popular one today. We are expected to be aggressive, to go out and get what we want when we want it. Those who wait patiently for the Lord to supply their needs are generally subject to ridicule.

The same is true in marriage. When we demand something from our spouse that he or she cannot deliver immediately, our first reaction is to turn away, to not be patient. If the disappointments and the turning away become habitual, our marriage is in deep trouble. Notice that the verse above does not say we will always get what we want. Instead, it promises that our hearts will be strengthened. We will learn to be patient—we will learn how to love—even when we do not receive what we think we want.

Lord, give us patience in the face of unmet needs, strengthen our hearts, and help us to wait on You.

CHANGE, CHANGE, CHANGE

*Jesus Christ is the same
yesterday, today, and forever.*

HEBREWS 13:8 NKJV

C hange ambushes us all. Just when we think we know someone as deeply as possible, we may wake up one morning and wonder who is on the other side of the bed. It certainly isn't the person we married! The problem is, we may not like a particular facet of his or her personality that didn't show itself until now.

People change as they go through life, sometimes for the better and sometimes not. A person—or a marriage—that does not grow or change is in trouble. Don't let change frighten you. As you age, change usually leads to a better life for you both. Only Jesus is the same "yesterday, today, and forever."

Father, we can see each other changing as our relationship progresses and are uncertain how the changes will work out. Sometimes this frightens us. Give us the courage we need to welcome change and adapt to it so we will both be free to become the people You mean us to be.

GIVE IN WITH A SMILE

A continual dripping
on a very rainy day
and a contentious woman are alike.

PROVERBS 27:15 NKJV

Lazily lying in bed on the weekend, have you ever been tormented by a constant drip from a leaky rain gutter? You drift off to sleep only to be jarred awake by the next drop. Will it never end? You take your pillow and stretch out on the couch, but you can still hear it. It's just farther away now.

Sometimes people irritate you the same way. Your husband or wife has a bone to pick with you, usually over something inconsequential such as mowing the lawn or going food shopping. For some reason, your spouse feels immediate action is required and just won't let it go. *Drip, drip, drip!* The only way to escape the irritation is to mow the lawn and fix the drip. Yes, those we love can drive us buggy, and two people can disagree on what is important. When that happens to you, do you have the grace to give in with a smile and bring peace to the family?

Father, when we get on each other's nerves, give us both the patience we need to deal with the problem and stop nagging each other. If something is that vital to our spouse, we need to be able to give in with a smile.

THE PEACE OF JESUS

"Peace I leave with you;
my peace I give you.
I do not give to you as the world gives.
Do not let your hearts be troubled
and do not be afraid."

JOHN 14:27 NIV

The couple that shares a belief in Jesus also shares the peace of Jesus—and the mystery of that peace. On the surface such a couple may not seem to have anything but trouble, yet they are happy and content, willing to share the little they do have. As Jesus told His disciples, He does not give as the world gives, but He does give peace.

Unbelievers who see such a couple are mystified. It makes no sense to them how, lacking in material possessions, two people can be at peace and living full, happy lives. For unbelievers the mystery will never be solved. But for Christians there is no secret to such a couple's happiness.

Father, sometimes the simplest gifts are too complex to comprehend. Whenever possible, help us share the secret of our contentment with those who do not understand Your peace and blessings.

ANSWERED PRAYER

"And I will do whatever
you ask in my name,
so that the Son may bring glory to the Father.
You may ask me for anything in my name,
and I will do it."

JOHN 14:13–14 NIV

Sometimes we forget what the real aim of our prayers should be. Jesus said we may ask for anything, spiritual or temporal, but often our prayers sound like the Christmas wish list of a young child. We may ask for a better job, release from suffering, and peace, all of which we are entitled to ask for, and much of which we will receive.

But when our prayers are answered, what do we do? We give thanks in private, because whose business is it what we have prayed for and received? But Jesus says prayers are answered only for one reason: so that His actions on our behalf will bring glory to the Father. Do we give God the glory when our prayers are answered, or do we keep it to ourselves?

Lord, You see to it that our prayers, big and small, are answered every day. When they are, give us the courage to openly give You the credit for our success.

Lean on Me

*"If the world hates you,
keep in mind that it hated me first."*

John 15:18 NIV

Maybe hate is too strong a word. Still, some days it seems that the world—or at least one person—is highly disappointed by how we turned out. We can't do anything right. And by the time the day is over, we're ready to call it quits and go to sleep.

There's no such thing as a new way of suffering, and you are not the first to feel hated, persecuted, or abandoned. When you feel that the whole world is against you, keep in mind that it first hated Jesus, God's only Son. And when He felt the hate of the world, Jesus just went on forgiving those who hated Him.

You are not alone. You have your spouse to lean on in times of trouble, as well as the One who was hated before you were even born.

Lord, thank You for giving me a loving companion to help me in days of trouble. Thank You for showing us how to deal with those who treat us poorly.

HOPE

"Now is your time of grief,
but I will see you again
and you will rejoice,
and no one will take away your joy."

JOHN 16:22 NIV

While grief comes in many forms, it is always related to some type of loss. A mother crying as she leaves her child at school on the first day of kindergarten is suffering from grief, even if she doesn't recognize the emotion. A soldier leaving his family behind, as well as those being left at home, will suffer grief. Even the act of moving to a new house or town, or having friends move away, will cause us real pain. The worst kind of grief, and the most lasting, is the pain we feel when someone we love dies.

A Christian family will suffer as much grief as any other family. Loss will hurt them just as deeply. The difference is, a Christian's grief is always tempered by hope. The loved one is still gone, but we have the hope of meeting again in heaven and experiencing permanent joy.

Father, when grief comes to us, be with us in our suffering and remind us of the joy that will be ours forever.

MOM AND DAD

*A fool despiseth
his father's instruction:
but he that regardeth reproof
is prudent.*

PROVERBS 15:5 KJV

You're married, supporting yourself and your family the best you can, and still your parents are giving you unsolicited advice! Will they never let you lead your own life?

Why in the world would you want them to do that? Consider that, aside from your spouse and God, they know you better than anyone, and they always have your best interests at heart. Who else will love you no matter what you say or do?

Your parents' advice may not always be perfect, but at least it is given in love and with no strings attached. Besides, as time goes by, you may even see that Mom and Dad were more often right than wrong!

Father, when I refuse to listen to my parents' advice, the only fool in the room is me. Give me the sense at least to listen and consider what they say, the way I do when my friends offer their advice.

Hold Your Tongue

A fool's wrath is presently known:
but a prudent man covereth shame.

PROVERBS 12:16 KJV

No matter how much we love our partners, there are times when they upset us or even cause us shame. We are still two different people—sometimes very different—and what would not bother one in the least can cause the other to fly into a rage. It takes time to explore and define emotional boundaries and to realize how far an argument can be carried before reason leaves the conversation and emotions take over.

Proverbs warns us to hold our tongues and not lash out at each other. Give your emotions time to subside; go for a drive or take a walk alone. Know that once you say the words you know will hurt your spouse the most, there is no taking them back, and the hurt you inflict could last for years.

Father, I know very well how to hurt my partner, to find that one weak spot that is the tenderest and most vulnerable. When I am feeling hurt and unloved, give me the self-control not to say the words that will hurt the most.

GOD BLESS. . .

Confess your faults one to another,
and pray one for another,
that ye may be healed.
The effectual fervent prayer
of a righteous man availeth much.

JAMES 5:16 KJV

Remember when you were a child you prayed the same prayer every evening before going to sleep? "God bless Mommy and Daddy and. . ." If you weren't ready to go to sleep yet, you could drag that list on forever. Now you may look back on that simple prayer and laugh at its innocence, but who can say that those prayers were not fervent or deny they could have made a difference in someone's life?

Do you pray as regularly for your spouse as you once did for your parents and other family members? Your world is certainly more complex, as are your prayers, but taking time to ask God to bless the one you love might be the most important thing you can do for your marriage.

Father, remind me that there is someone close to me who needs and deserves my prayers every day.

RECONCILIATION

Be ye angry, and sin not:
let not the sun go down
upon your wrath.

EPHESIANS 4:26 KJV

There's nothing more depressing than a two-day argument. If you go to sleep angry, you toss and turn all night because you know you'll only wake up in the middle of the same old fight. It's depressing to start the day with both of you at the extreme edges of the same bed. True, not every disagreement can be settled in one day, but there is no need to go to bed upset and angry.

No matter what the issue, you do have other things you agree on. Before you go to sleep, talk about the children, an upcoming vacation, or something good that happened at work. Tell your spouse you love him or her, and agree to disagree for the time being. Sometimes this reconciliation will be easy, and sometimes it will seem forced and insincere, but either way you need to go to sleep at peace with each other.

Father, we share so much as a couple that it's foolish to let a disagreement ruin the whole day. When we are arguing, remind us how much we love each other and give us the strength to make peace.

LOVE AND RESPECT

*Let every one of you
in particular
so love his wife even as himself;
and the wife see that she
reverence her husband.*

EPHESIANS 5:33 KJV

Mutual respect is the foundation of a good marriage. Two different people may have legitimate opposing views on any subject, from how to handle money to which football team to support. Of importance is not the issue but how you treat each other.

The wife of Ephesians 5:33 is not being told to worship her husband and leave all the decisions to him. Only God deserves to be worshiped; only God never makes mistakes. She is told to respect her husband and give his views a fair, loving hearing. The husband is told to love his wife at least as much as he loves himself. That means he must respect her and give her views the same fair and loving hearing he expects for himself.

Don't fall into the "I'm in charge here" trap. You need each other's viewpoints to successfully handle the troubles that will come your way.

Father, You are in charge of our marriage. You gave us each other as a gift of happiness. Don't let our egos destroy that happiness.

THE GOLDEN RULE

So in everything,
do to others what you would
have them do to you,
for this sums up
the Law and the Prophets.

MATTHEW 7:12 NIV

Treat someone badly and you can expect he'll return the favor. Often he won't stop a second before retaliating. Treat a person well and you may have earned yourself a life-long friend. It's a trait of human nature to give as good as we get.

The truth of the Golden Rule works for us or against us in marriage. Even the most devoted spouse gets fed up with continual bad treatment, but few can resist someone who treats them with respect and consideration.

When your wife has a brutal workday and wants to order takeout food, do you dump on her about family finances, or do you offer to make dinner instead? When your husband doesn't feel like driving, do you offer to take the wheel?

Treating your spouse with consideration builds up your marriage and the friendship it's founded on. Following the Golden Rule could lead you to a golden anniversary.

Lord, we want to treat each other well for a lifetime, not just occasionally. Give us the grace to treat each other well every day.

THOSE ROUGH SPOTS

*For there is not a word
on my tongue, but behold, O LORD,
You know it altogether.*

PSALM 139:4 NKJV

The married couple doesn't exist that hasn't exchanged words that shouldn't have been spoken. Occasionally we all open our mouths and cause distress. The moment we see the hurt those words caused, we may blurt out, "I'm sorry, I didn't mean that." Yet we writhe under the knowledge that words don't erase the pain.

Nothing, not even harsh words, are beyond God's knowledge and forgiveness. So why doesn't God stop us in midsentence? Couldn't He keep us from such sin?

Of course God could. But then the sinful attitudes and thoughts we harbor inside would remain a mystery. We'd never understand the hidden frustrations that work on our innermost parts.

When we let our mouths flap, we see ourselves as we really are—believers with rough spots. As God refines those rough spots in our love for Him, our mates can see a new love shine. Then our marriages truly reflect how we feel about the greatest Lover.

Lord God, thank You that no harsh words of ours can destroy Your love for us. Make our lives reflect that love.

MIRROR GOD'S MERCY

And forgive us our debts,
as we forgive our debtors.

MATTHEW 6:12 KJV

Your spouse hurt you deeply. Whether words darted into your soul or an action offended you, your heart aches.

What do you do? Holding a grudge may seem okay for a while, but where does it get you? Giving the silent treatment or needling your spouse only ruins communication and eventually destroys a marriage.

Maybe you need to wrestle with that pain. Take the time to understand why your husband or wife caused you anguish. But dwelling on the wrong won't ease the situation. Sooner or later—and the sooner, the better—you need to forgive that injury.

Accept that your spouse is human, makes mistakes, and falls victim to sin. Understand how much both of you need God's forgiveness and that you need to mirror His mercy in your married life.

Forgiveness isn't a one-way street. Tomorrow you may do something thoughtless and be looking for the same "no strings attached" pardon. You'll be glad it's there.

Lord God, thank You for not holding a grudge against us for our sin. Help us forgive as You have forgiven us.

Godly Goals

Therefore,
since Christ suffered in his body,
arm yourselves also with the same attitude,
because he who has suffered in his body is done with sin.
As a result, he does not live the rest of
his earthly life for evil human desires,
but rather for the will of God.

1 Peter 4:1–2 niv

God forgives us for sins great and small. Nothing is too large or inconsequential for His mercy.

Because the price He paid for that mercy was His only Son, Jesus, God takes forgiveness seriously. He doesn't see forgiveness as something to sweep under the rug. He expects those who have been forgiven to be willing to change their lifestyles.

Those changes should influence our marriages, too. Instead of making our spouses suffer for our selfishness, we should become increasingly sensitive to our mates. When we wrong each other, we ought to ask for and offer forgiveness as quickly as possible. Our evil desires will decline as our godly goals increase.

Can you imagine a more "perfect" marriage than being wed to a spouse like that?

Lord Jesus, You suffered to bring us freedom from sin; help us to live to know and do Your will each day.

ROMANTIC LOVE

*Your love is
more delightful than wine.*

SONG OF SOLOMON 1:2 NIV

Anyone who thinks God has no romance in His makeup is dead wrong. It only takes a peek at the Song of Solomon to see that God invented romance. This short, powerful book describes the passionate outpouring of God's emotions on those who believe in Him.

Though it describes the relationship between God and His people, the Song of Solomon has much to say to husbands and wives. God designed marriage to be a delightful experience shared by a man and woman. The power of wedded bliss to intoxicate goes far beyond wine yet lacks wine's harmful properties.

There's no church holiday for romantic love, but Valentine's Day is a good time to remember how much your spouse means to you and to appreciate the love God has given you.

Be intoxicated with each other, without even taking a sip of wine!

Thank You, Father God, for showing us the joy of married love. Help us to take time today to express the depth of emotion that we share.

Living for Heaven

*A kindhearted woman
gains respect,
but ruthless men gain only wealth.*

Proverbs 11:16 NIV

In the workplace you may have run into one of those hard-hitting types who has a bundle of money but is despised by everyone. He thinks no one can see through his machinations, but most know he can't be trusted.

Maybe his wife is a kind, gentle soul whom everyone loves. Though her husband hasn't a clue, the only reason he gets invited anywhere socially is because people respect her enough to be too embarrassed not to let him tag along.

In this world he may seem like the big cheese because he owns a company, a yacht, and real estate. But in heaven people may be surprised to find that she has a place of honor, while he has disappeared into insignificance.

Today, are you living for heaven or only to acquire earthly possessions?

Keep us mindful of Your truth, Father God, as we live from day to day. Let our bank account be of service to You instead of a sign of our disobedience.

THOSE NECESSARY THORNS

Therefore I will block
her path with thornbushes;
I will wall her in so that
she cannot find her way.

HOSEA 2:6 NIV

Gomer, the prophet Hosea's wife, had fallen into serious sin by seeking the affections of other men. So God made a promise to Hosea. Life wouldn't turn out the way Gomer had expected, and trouble would make her return to Hosea.

Even though we have been faithful, we might empathize with Gomer. There we are, living each day, everything organized and neat, when *wham!* life starts falling apart. Suddenly our spouses seem about a mile away, and troubles multiply. While things are going along fine, we can't see that we begin to depend on ourselves, forget the needs of our mates, and leave less and less time in our days for God.

Sometimes we all need "thornbushes" to get us right with our mates and Maker. When the stickers prick our skin, we recognize how much we need God—and our spouses—and start reorganizing our lives to reflect that.

God can move thornbushes, not just mountains!

Thank You, Lord, for bringing thornbushes into our lives to show us when we're stuck. Draw us closer to You and to each other, before we reach those bushes.

GIVING EXTRAVAGANTLY

He who did not spare His own Son,
but delivered Him up for us all,
how shall He not with Him
also freely give us all things?

ROMANS 8:32 NKJV

To love is to give. If someone says, "I love you," but won't help you out or give in other ways, chances are that person isn't really loving. Together, you won't have much of a relationship.

God not only gives to us, He gives extravagantly. He offered up His Son, the dearest thing He had to give. Anything else seems small in comparison. And God keeps on giving good gifts—and only good gifts—all the time.

To have a happy marital relationship also means giving: time, effort, forgiveness, and that special every-morning kiss. It also means occasionally giving physical gifts: a how-to video he's wanted for a long time, or a rose to tell her she's special. Whether it's a helping hand or a wrapped-up package, each gift shows your spouse you know what he or she needs and that you care for that need.

What need can you fill for your spouse today?

Father God, thank You for loving us so much that You gave us just what we needed—Your Son, Jesus. We want to show love to each other by giving good gifts, too.

Time for Togetherness

But a married man is concerned
about the affairs of this world—
how he can please his wife. . . .
But a married woman is concerned
about the affairs of this world—
how she can please her husband.

1 Corinthians 7:33–34 niv

Before you marry you can do as you please, spiritually and in other ways. But once you commit to your spouse, you have to take that person into consideration. Paul was just pointing out the obvious—someone with his challenging ministry in the face of persecution had to choose between God and marriage.

If you think you can spend all your time at work or on a ministry, think again. It isn't fair to give your spouse only the late-night hours when you're wiped out from a hectic day. You won't communicate clearly under those conditions, and arguments are likely to come more often and fiercely.

Married couples need time together, uninterrupted by children, work, or family chores. Whether it's regular date nights or a few hours set aside for morning devotions and talk, schedule time to share. Your spouse will be pleased to no end.

Lord, we often lose track of our need to spend time together without distractions. Help us to please each other, and not just our bosses.

Firm Foundations

The contentions of a wife
are a continual dripping.

Proverbs 19:13 nkjv

Drip, drip, drip, what an irritating sound! You'd do almost anything to stop it. Maybe that's why so many use the "driplike" technique of nagging to try to get their way.

But nagging isn't a productive way to deal with problems. It just irritates one's spouse and shows the nagger's foolishness. After a while the nagged mate just ignores the scolding and goes his or her own way.

Nagging can serve a useful purpose, though, if both spouses treat it as a warning signal. When your spouse keeps mentioning the same concern or situation, it's time to wake up and realize that you need to deal with something here.

Maybe you need to call in a plumber or carpenter to fix something in the house, or maybe you need to discuss an aspect of your marriage. Whatever it is, stop that leak before it floats your marriage off its foundations.

Lord, we don't want to turn into a pair of naggers. Give us the wisdom to solve our problems before they float us away.

CATCH THE FOXES

Catch us the foxes,
the little foxes that spoil the vines,
for our vines have tender grapes.

SONG OF SOLOMON 2:15 NKJV

Often it isn't big things that make a marriage uncomfortable. Rather, it's the little, picky problems that may disturb an otherwise happy relationship. Just a touch of an unforgiving attitude here or a lack of consideration there can make you wake up grumpy in the morning and carry an unsettled feeling through the day. You bark at coworkers and your spouse and don't even realize why.

Those small annoyances are like little foxes plundering the grapes in the vineyard. They may not ruin the vines, but they sure impact the crop. Just as the hardworking farmer begins to wonder if he's in the business of feeding foxes or growing grapes, you start wondering who escaped with the joy that once flooded your marriage.

To make sure your marriage goes well, catch the foxes of bitterness, lack of forgiveness, and irritation before they ruin your joy.

Lord God, we don't want a loveless marriage that gives no testimony to You. We want to keep the troubles in our relationship small by coming to You with even the small sins.

ONLY A PRAYER AWAY

But I am poor and needy; make haste to me, O God!
You are my help and my deliverer;
O LORD, do not delay.

PSALM 70:5 NKJV

Whether you need money to pay the bills or answers on how to deal with balky teenagers, you've probably prayed a "Help, quick!" prayer to God. Everyone has those moments when nothing on earth, not even our much-loved spouses, seems to answer the need. Only God is big enough for this trouble.

There's no weakness in coming to God when we need help. It isn't wrong to ask for assistance in our marriage or relationships or even for our earthly needs. David knew that when he asked God not to let his enemies kill him. The soon-to-be king knew God wanted to hear about all his troubles.

God loves to hear all our prayers, even the ones that begin "Help, quick!" When we see an out-of-control SUV hurtling down the road toward us, when we enter a crowded emergency room with a seriously ill loved one, or when we just don't know what to say in response to someone's critical words, God is only a prayer away.

Whenever we need deliverance, He's there to care. We just need to be humble enough to ask.

Thank You, Father God, that You hear our every prayer. Give us humble hearts to ask for our every need.

TRANSFORMED

And in the house his disciples asked him again of the same matter.
And he saith unto them,
Whosoever shall put away his wife, and marry another,
committeth adultery against her.

MARK 10:10–11 KJV

The disciples didn't feel comfortable knowing a person might have to stick with a marriage that didn't appear to have a terrific future. Not much has changed since the first century.

Few of us like to close out divorce. We'd rather think there's a "back door" we can sneak out if things get rough. Our sin nature hates unrestricted commitment.

Try to stick to marital responsibilities solely under your own power and you will look for a back door, because any sin-filled person has a tough time remaining faithful. But you slam that back door and lock it when you allow God free rein in your marriage. Though you can't ignore marital problems, thinking they'll solve themselves, you can overcome them with God's strength. When His Spirit fills your marriage, you'll avoid some troubles. Instead of despairing, you grow through the trials. As you conform to His likeness, your lives are transformed, and marriage becomes better.

And *that's* a terrific future.

Lord Jesus, Your words may not be easy to accept, but we know You will help us follow them. Fill us with Your Spirit so we can be conformed to Your likeness.

LOVE QUALITIES

What is desired
in a man is kindness,
and a poor man is better than a liar.

PROVERBS 19:22 NKJV

What qualities did you see in your partner that made you decide, This is the one? Was it passion or politeness? wealth or wisdom? success or steadfastness? Although the qualities in the verse above seem very different from those admired by our culture, they are probably close to what your mother told you to look for in a mate. Kindness, truthfulness, faithfulness, patience, and joyfulness—all the attributes of a good Christian—make for a good spouse.

Don't let the media convince you that there is something missing in your partner because she's a little overweight or he is developing a bald spot on the top of his head. On those days when your spouse is obviously less than perfect, remember why you fell in love in the first place.

Father, neither of us is perfect by today's standards. But it was Your standards that attracted us to each other and will keep us together for the rest of our lives.

LOVING TRUTH

But, speaking the truth in love. . . .

EPHESIANS 4:15 NKJV

There are two ways to speak the truth: in love and not in love. Some couples vow never to keep the truth from each other, no matter what. Others are more foresighted, realizing that the brutal truth is not always what people want or need to hear.

"How do I look in this dress?" has only one acceptable answer: "You look absolutely wonderful!"

"Am I going bald?" does not deserve an absolutely truthful answer either. "You're more handsome than ever" will do nicely.

It's not that you are lying when you sidestep this type of question. Your husband does think you look wonderful, and you do think he's more handsome than ever. You just didn't answer the question the way it was posed. The point is, you are speaking the truth—in love.

Father, we realize that the truth is the best answer but not when it would hurt the one we love. Help us to speak the truth with love.

LOVING DISAGREEMENTS

Not rendering evil for evil,
or railing for railing:
but contrariwise blessing;
knowing that ye are thereunto called,
that ye should inherit a blessing.

1 PETER 3:9 KJV

A couple made up of two strong personalities is sure to have an interesting life together, to say the least. There will be more bumps in their marriage than for two more laid-back mates. This is not in itself a problem as long as both know how to handle disagreements in a loving manner.

Strong-willed people attack problems with determination, overcome them, and then go on to the next task. What may at first seem to be a weakness in their relationship can turn out to be a blessing.

Father, two strong people do not have to pull in opposite directions. When they pull together, with Your help, they can move mountains. Remind us of that the next time we disagree.

QUIET TIMES

Live joyfully with the wife
whom thou lovest.

ECCLESIASTES 9:9 KJV

A young couple committed to each other often finds marriage to be a lot of work. The first few years are a time of adjustment and compromise, a time to settle the basic issues. Then you may decide to have children, with all the work that entails. As your family grows, so do your bills, and you work harder and longer.

Don't let all the issues and the children and the stress destroy the joy that comes with marriage. Never be too busy to enjoy quiet times with your spouse, to laugh or play like the children you once were together. Keep your relationship young and happy. In time, your children will grow up and leave, and once again it will be just the two of you. Will you find that you and your spouse are strangers, or will you greet that time of your life with joy? It all depends on what you do now.

Father, remind us how to play and how to enjoy being with each other. Help us remain best friends and lovers throughout our lives.

HAPPY IN LOVE

*Thou hast put gladness
in my heart.*

PSALM 4:7 KJV

Somewhere, sometime, a friend or relative has probably asked you, "What do you see in that person?"

You can go to great lengths to answer the question, ticking off one point after another until your questioner caves in and backs off. Or you can become angry and lash out in reply, which will make you feel better but doesn't answer the question.

The next time someone asks such a tactless question, avoid both explanation and anger by quietly saying, "She [He] makes me happy." Even the most critical of people will admit (at least in their hearts) that there is no comeback to that answer.

Lord, You have given us each other because You knew we would make each other happy. In an unhappy world, that is one of the greatest gifts of all.

First Place

Listen, my son,
to your father's instruction
and do not forsake
your mother's teaching.

Proverbs 1:8 niv

You have been listening to your father and mother all your life, but now you are half of a couple, dedicated to making your relationship last and grow. There will be times when your spouse must come first, when you will have to put his or her wishes ahead of those of your parents. Wise parents understand this and don't take it personally when you put your spouse first, but sometimes they still need to put in their two cents' worth.

How do you handle this type of conflict? Very carefully! Your parents must accept that you are no longer just their child but also a husband or wife and that your spouse's wishes must take first place in your decisions. At the same time, you must accept that your parents still have a lot they can teach you, and you owe them your respect. Welcome their input whenever possible, thank them for their love and care, and then do what you have to do. They'll understand.

Father, give us the love and tactfulness we need in situations like this so no one is hurt or disappointed and we all remain "family."

WORTHY OF TRUST

It is better to trust in the LORD
than to put confidence in man.
It is better to trust in the LORD
than to put confidence in princes.

PSALM 118:8–9 NKJV

Two of the most dangerous words in the English language are "trust me." Whoever says this is asking you to suspend your natural intelligence and avoid asking the hard questions. Whoever says this may be placing you in financial or personal danger or even pitting you against your spouse. If you're in the military, you don't have much choice in the matter. Otherwise, following someone blindly is an act of stupidity, whether you're being asked to trust a used car salesman or a politician.

Being married to a sensible person is a great defense. One of you may be fooled, but it's harder to fool two people at the same time. If your spouse has doubts when you are asked to trust someone other than the Lord, pay attention to his or her wariness, ask some tough questions, and be very sure the person in question is worthy of your trust.

Father, we know You are the only one who deserves our complete confidence. Give us the discernment we need and show us what we should do when we are asked to follow someone else.

Anytime, Anyplace Worship

Therefore glorify the LORD
in the dawning light.

Isaiah 24:15 NKJV

It's hard to glorify God while concentrating on shaving or trying to get everyone up and out on time. No one has time for more than the bare essentials at dawn, but the beginning of a new day is a precious gift that should be welcomed and for which we should give thanks. How can a couple find time for this when they can't even sit down and eat breakfast together?

We tend to think of worship as an institutional event, but it doesn't always have to be so. You can pray for your children as you pack their lunches or sing a doxology in the shower. Opening the blinds and feeling the sun cross your face can be a religious experience, as can watching your children climb onto the school bus, filled with expectations of a good day.

You don't always need a congregation to worship; it's enough that God hears your thanksgiving for this day.

Father, we do appreciate the blessing of each new day. Make Yourself such a constant presence in our lives that we are able to worship You at any place, in any situation.

Everything from God

When times are good, be happy;
but when times are bad, consider:
God has made the one
as well as the other.

Ecclesiastes 7:14 NIV

No one expects us to be cheerful and happy in the face of bad times. We may be Christians, but we bleed and cry just as much as nonbelievers.

You probably know at least one couple that has gone through terrible suffering with tremendous faith and fortitude. How do they cope? What do they know that you don't? More than likely, they have taken to heart the second part of the above verse: "When times are bad, consider: God has made the one as well as the other." Good and bad, happy and sad, everything comes from God. We may not like some of the things He gives us, but He has His own reasons beyond our understanding, and everything is part of His plan.

Father, it's hard to give thanks for pain. Grant us the wisdom to accept Your plan for our lives, even when it hurts, for we know everything comes from You.

Right Turns, Right Path

And thine ears shall hear
a word behind thee, saying,
This is the way, walk ye in it,
when ye turn to the right hand,
and when ye turn to the left.

Isaiah 30:21 KJV

Notice that this verse doesn't say you'll never wander off the right path. Our desire to go smell the flowers elsewhere can be overwhelming, as can our sheer stubbornness. "It's only a little detour," one might say. "I can get back on the right path anytime I want. I know exactly where it is."

If you've ever done any wilderness hiking, you know how dangerous wandering off the path can be and how easily you can get turned around and lost. Right now you and your spouse are hiking through life together. That's good, because hiking alone can be scary, not to mention dangerous. You need to listen when your spouse has misgivings about a turn you want to take. You need to consult each other, read the map God has provided, and not allow yourselves to be tempted off the path and into the wilderness.

Father, whenever one of us hears Your warning voice, make the other take the alarm seriously. Help us not to continue on the wrong path, trusting more in ourselves than in You.

REJOICING

May your fountain be blessed,
and may you rejoice in
the wife of your youth.

PROVERBS 5:18 NIV

Marriage takes a lot of work," you'll hear people say, until you wonder if they're planning a forty-hour work week for marriage, on top of your career.

If by "work" they mean you have to treat each other well, settle differences, and stick together through the hard times, perhaps they're right. But if they mean that marriage is just drudgery, nothing could be further from God's truth.

God didn't make marriage to be painful. He wants to give two people an opportunity to serve Him, enjoy each other, and share happiness and troubles. When we put Him first in our marriages and follow His rules for love, we rejoice in our spouses. Even when we face trouble, God's grace lifts us up and enables us to take delight in our mates.

Are you rejoicing today?

Lord, we don't want our marriage to be drudgery. If we aren't rejoicing, show us where we need to draw closer to You so we can come nearer to each other.

A Fine-Tuned Machine

*Be kind and
compassionate to one another,
forgiving each other,
just as in Christ God forgave you.*

EPHESIANS 4:32 NIV

When one mate holds a grudge against the other, the signs of conflict radiate from both partners.

A marriage without kindness, compassion, and forgiveness lacks the oil that makes a relationship run smoothly. Because grudges remain and are constantly pointed out, a load of "sand" has destroyed a fine-tuned machine. Suddenly its engine grinds to a halt. What you have isn't a relationship anymore—it's a wreck.

The damage probably began with sin. Undoubtedly, there was something the hurt partner "just couldn't" forgive. Instead of seeking resolution, the couple took the easy way out and traded hurtful barbs. Kindness and compassion went to the side, and emotional sniping took its place.

If your relationship has sand in it, wash it out with forgiveness and fill it with kindness and compassion. Don't turn your marriage into a broken-down engine but into a fine-tuned machine for God.

Lord, we don't want to battle each other instead of Satan. Show us how to make forgiveness, kindness, and compassion flow in our marriage.

GENTLE CORRECTION

"Or how can you say to your brother,
'Let me remove the speck from your eye';
and look, a plank is in your own eye? . . .
First remove the plank from your own eye."

MATTHEW 7:4–5 NKJV

Two people sharing a marriage have plenty of opportunity to see each other's flaws.

Sometimes we have to hold each other to account and suggest a change. To fail to do so would be to treat marriage irresponsibly. Not surprisingly, a mate may not respond well to that information.

So, before you point out anything, ask yourself if you've contributed to the situation. If you have, start by asking forgiveness from God and your mate. Then be aware of the sensitive places in your spouse's heart. Forgiveness, not harsh criticism, needs to cushion your discussion.

Finally, change doesn't come easily to any of us, and it may take time. A correcting partner also needs to be a patient partner.

Thank You, God, that through You, we can make changes in our lives. Help us to be sensitive to each other when we need to correct or be corrected.

A CLOSE SECOND

*Then went in also
that other disciple,
which came first to the sepulchre,
and he saw, and believed.*

JOHN 20:8 KJV

For three years John had followed Jesus. Then, in one divine moment, the truth connected, and suddenly the disciple knew that this was Messiah, the one for whom his heart had searched.

Meeting the right man or woman and "just clicking" can seem delightful. You've never experienced such intimacy, and you marry. But even a satisfying marriage pales beside knowing Jesus truly and deeply.

Through Him we understand ourselves and each other more clearly. Jesus cleans out the dirty spaces in our hearts and gives us true joy. He can make marriage wonderful, but no marriage—even one provided and blessed by Him—can fill the places He fills in our hearts.

Nothing on this earth is truly divine, no matter how much we enjoy it. Nothing, not even a much-loved spouse, can take the place of God in our hearts.

Give Jesus first place in your heart and award your spouse a close second. Then you both will win.

Thank You, Lord, for blessing us with this marriage. But remind us daily that we are not "number one," You are.

THE POSITIVE STUFF

And Peter answered unto her,
Tell me whether
ye sold the land for so much?
And she said, Yea, for so much. . . .
Peter said. . .How is it that ye have agreed
together to tempt the Spirit of the Lord?

ACTS 5:8–9 KJV

Ananias and Sapphira may not have agreed on much in their marriage. Maybe they constantly argued over the household expenses, or maybe they had different goals for their income. But when it came to lying to the apostles about the price they got for land they sold, the two spoke as a single voice. Even when Peter caught them in a lie, neither admitted the sin or asked forgiveness. The spiritual death that gripped them cost the two their lives.

Some husbands and wives seem to find agreement on the wrong things; the partners think lying, infidelity, and other sins are fine—as long as they don't get caught. Those attitudes don't kill the couple off as rapidly as Ananias and Sapphira's did, but they are signs of spiritual death.

Christian marriages need to find agreement on many positive things: truths we recognize, family goals, and ways in which we can honor God. Are you in agreement today to honor God?

Lord, give us good agreement in our marriage.

TEAMWORK

. . .Submitting yourselves
one to another in the fear of God.

EPHESIANS 5:21 KJV

Put two people together as husband and wife and either teamwork or a pulling contest results.

Teamwork isn't a matter of one partner driving the other but of two pulling in the direction God has set for them. As they move in the same direction, in service to Him, they take each other into consideration. And that marriage grows.

Working as a team isn't always easy. Sometimes one team member becomes a "hot dog," trying to take all the glory; then the other member feels unimportant, and trouble ensues. At other times both members of the team go off in their own directions. Neither is productive.

But a smoothly working team that submits to the needs of each other is wonderful to watch. It has a set goal, and the partners work in rhythm to accomplish it. When they seek to obey God, His will is done, and He is glorified.

In what direction is your marriage going?

A pulling contest isn't what we want our marriage to be, Lord.
Today head us in the direction You have for our shared lives.

The Third Cord

*A threefold cord is not
quickly broken.*

ECCLESIASTES 4:12 KJV

Working things out on your own can get tiring. Without the advice and strength of another, making decisions and directing your life can become wearying. When your spouse comes alongside to help, it can be a great blessing.

But even when together you head in the same direction and serve God with all your hearts, you can come to a roadblock. Neither of you can see the future. Should you spend money on redoing the house, because you'll eventually sell it for more, or should you bank that money for another need?

That's why it's important to have a third cord in your strand of decision making: God. Alone, you can make a devastating wrong choice. But when the Lord of time and space is at the center of your choices, even those that seem less than perfect will turn out fine.

One alone works hard and two are better. But the perfect solution is two relying on the One.

Thank You, Lord, that You care about our choices and want to help us make good ones. Be the center of every decision we make.

SPIRITUAL GIFTS

There are diversities of gifts,
but the same Spirit.
There are differences of ministries,
but the same Lord.

1 CORINTHIANS 12:4–5 NKJV

God gifts each of His people with spiritual abilities that serve the church and the world. Some are wonderful preachers, others provide strong testimonies, while still others offer comfort to hurting spirits.

This diversity of gifts could hardly be contained in one person. Who would have time to do every good work or be in every place at the same time? That's why God gave gifts to each Christian.

Every marriage contains a collection of spiritual gifts. A wife may be a great comforter, while her husband easily reaches out to those in pain. Or a great preacher may marry a great organizer who helps keep their lives in order.

Those gifts aren't meant to start competition in a marriage, but to benefit others, including your mate. Both of you serve the same Lord, even if your gifts differ. You can use them to reach the world for Christ—or waste time arguing over which set of gifts is "better."

Lord, thank You for giving us gifts that are "best" in Your sight.
Help us to serve You faithfully with them.

STRENGTH IN DIVERSITY

O LORD, you have searched me and you know me. . . .
You are familiar with all my ways.

PSALM 139:1, 3 NIV

Before you were born God knew just what you would be like. Light skin or dark? Fair, straight hair or glossy dark ringlets? Easily tempted to become angry or one who goes with the flow?

You and your spouse grew up in homes with diverse family backgrounds. You came out of your environments as different people. Maybe one went to college while the other went straight to work.

You started dating and found common ground, but once you married, those differences cropped up again. *Can two such opposite people share the same marriage?* you might wonder.

Take heart. God didn't mean you to be duplicates.

Marital contrasts can strengthen that relationship if a couple shares them instead of treating each other's ideas as alien territory. Handled well, differing attitudes and abilities create a deeper relationship, not a battleground.

Don't fight over differences. Rather, deal lovingly and intelligently with them, and you'll develop a stronger marriage, fusing your strengths and limiting your weaknesses.

God knew you weren't identical—even twins aren't exactly the same!

Lord, help us understand our differences and use them to strengthen our marriage.

BUILDING TRUST

Ye shall not steal, neither deal falsely,
neither lie one to another.

LEVITICUS 19:11 KJV

Trustworthiness is the key to a good marriage. Without it, even the most loving of couples will have problems. But like all things that must be earned, to develop trustworthiness takes time.

Trust is built up during courtship. While no one sensible would marry someone he or she knows can't be trusted, there is a special type of trust that belongs to marriage. As you mature together, the trust between you becomes deeper.

Along the way you learn to call when you will be late for dinner, how to make coffee exactly the way your spouse likes it, and how to hold the baby properly. Then, somewhere along the line, the trust between you becomes absolute. Your husband lets you drive his new car without going through a litany of "do nots." Your wife lets you take the children camping for the weekend without checking to see that you packed everything you could possibly need. Finally, it dawns on you one day that this person would actually sacrifice his or her own life to save yours—without hesitation or second thoughts—and you would do the same for him or her.

That's a little frightening! That's trust.

Father, help us build trust in each other as the years go by, until we are totally comfortable with each other and know we have nothing to fear from the one we love.

FINANCE

Let no man seek his own,
but every man another's wealth.

1 CORINTHIANS 10:24 KJV

How do you as a couple handle your money? Do you own everything jointly, or do you each have your own checking and savings accounts? Do you have wills that reflect the realities of your lives and your responsibilities? Do you have enough insurance? Are you saving for your children's education and investing for your retirement?

The details of how you handle your money are important, but not as important as your attitude toward them. It's vital that you both agree to whatever arrangement you work out. Some wives will feel perfectly comfortable putting everything into joint accounts and letting their husbands handle everything. Others will feel nervous with such an arrangement. It's important that you discuss these matters with honesty and consideration for each other and come to mutually acceptable decisions.

Father, we both bring our own financial history into marriage and will disagree on some details. Help us come to an agreement that is based on love and consideration for each other.

SINGING HILLS

For ye shall go out with joy,
and be led forth with peace:
the mountains and the hills
shall break forth before you into singing,
and all the trees of the field
shall clap their hands.

ISAIAH 55:12 KJV

At first the idea of animated hills and trees may seem silly. But go back in your mind and recall the happiest moment of your life—your wedding day, the day your first child was born, or the day you accepted Jesus as your Lord. A day totally unlike any other. The sunlight was so bright, the air so clear! Can't you still feel the gentle touch of the breeze on your face, hear the songs of the birds, see the greenness of the grass and the dance of the trees? Your senses were more acute than ever before, and the whole world sang with you.

This is an earthly experience of the joy of the Lord, a joy so total and so amazing that you just want to laugh out loud and run in circles until you collapse. And who's to say the hills can't sing or the trees can't clap their hands on such a day?

Lord, You fill our lives with joy beyond our understanding, and we thank You for these precious times.

LAUGH AT THE REST

Who can discern his errors?
Forgive my hidden faults.

PSALM 19:12 NIV

You knew your spouse wasn't perfect when you married, but you didn't know he snored like an elephant! That's not one of the questions we generally ask before offering or accepting an engagement ring. On the other hand, you forgot to mention that you cut your toenails in the living room. What's the big deal?

Most of the things that drive us crazy in a marriage were never mentioned in advance. They are truly "hidden" faults, those things a person does without realizing they might bug another. Indeed, a snorer rarely hears his own snores and will vehemently deny that he snores at all. And if everyone in your family clipped their toenails in such a manner, you assumed it was perfectly normal behavior. Have patience with each other, change what can be changed, and laugh at the rest.

Father, when our hidden faults suddenly appear in our marriage, help us understand they are mostly harmless, unconscious habits. Help us change what can be changed and accept what cannot be changed.

LOVING SACRIFICE

Live a life of love,
just as Christ loved us
and gave himself up for us
as a fragrant offering
and sacrifice to God.

EPHESIANS 5:2 NIV

S acrifice is required in a marriage. Instead of playing in the Saturday morning baseball game, you stay home and cut the grass. Instead of going out to dinner on payday with the rest of your coworkers, you go home and relieve the baby-sitter. You may not be happy about giving up your fun, but you do—sometimes kicking and screaming—for the good of your marriage and family.

You may not say you are sacrificing for love. But that's the reason you do it: because of love. Your marriage is more important to you than a night out or a weekend game. You are living a life of love.

Father, marriage and family require sacrifices from both of us. Give us the grace to accept this, because sacrifice brings us closer and helps us grow as a family.

IMPERFECTIONS AND ALL

Many a man claims to
have unfailing love,
but a faithful man who can find?

PROVERBS 20:6 NIV

Is your love for your spouse perfect? Do you always act out of unfailing love? Of course not; you're human. Sometimes you speak sharply to your spouse, ignore your children, stomp out of the house in anger, or shut it all out in front of the TV. Anyone who expects unfailing love will probably have that notion dispelled before the honeymoon's over. Unfailing love belongs in songs and dreams, not in real life.

But that doesn't mean we should never love. How foolish it would be to look for the "perfect" mate when we ourselves are so imperfect. Instead of looking for the imperfections, concentrate on your mate's good qualities, the things that made you fall in love in the first place. Praise those qualities and thank God for bringing you together, imperfections and all.

Father, neither of us is perfect, and our love is a flawed human love. When we have problems, let us look to You as the example of perfect love we should aim for, even though we know we'll fall far short of the mark.

AGING

Cast me not off
in the time of old age;
forsake me not
when my strength faileth.

PSALM 71:9 KJV

Some wise person once noted that old age is not for sissies. Aging brings a whole new set of challenges that couples must learn to deal with, including the fear of abandonment. Neither of you is the same person you were thirty years ago. Hair goes gray or away, muscles migrate south, and you begin to fear you are no longer physically attractive to your spouse. Even though you trust your partner, you know you could never compete with a "youngster" of forty.

Well, your spouse has the same worries! If you've made it this far as a couple, your worries are most likely unfounded. Take time to reassure your spouse that your love has not lessened, just matured.

Father, help us adjust to our aging bodies and put away any fears we may have about our attractiveness and remind us to reassure each other of our love.

GRANDCHILDREN

*Children's children are
the crown of old men.*

PROVERBS 17:6 KJV

Being a grandparent is one of God's rewards for hanging in there and, at times, putting up with your children. Sure, you love your children, but they were, and always will be, a responsibility. Along with the joy they brought you came duties, worries, and obligations. With them, you had to do the right thing, day after day, for over twenty years.

Grandchildren, on the other hand, are pure, unadulterated joy. They expect nothing of you, and when you get tired, you can send them home. You can buy them expensive toys without worrying about spoiling them. When they ask difficult questions, you may be surprised to discover that you actually know the answers. They will love you if you fall asleep in the middle of their bedtime story, laugh at your stupidest joke, and be happy to see you whenever you appear on their doorstep.

And there is yet another benefit: All the emotional baggage between you and your children is thrown away the minute you see your first grandchild.

Lord, our grandchildren are a taste of immortality to come, and we thank You for blessing us with their presence.

A HIGHER AUTHORITY

Labour not to be rich;
cease from thine own wisdom.
Wilt thou set thine eyes upon
that which is not?
for riches certainly make
themselves wings;
they fly away as
an eagle toward heaven.

PROVERBS 23:4–5 KJV

The last time you had to write a check for your federal taxes, did you notice that instead of making it payable to the Internal Revenue Service you now pay the U.S. Treasury? It may be just a public relations ploy on the part of the government, but it's a good one. We've all been promoted and now report to someone higher, which somehow makes writing that check a little easier.

We have the option of reporting to a higher authority in all financial matters. Each couple decides how to handle their own finances: how much to spend, save, invest, and donate. Very few of us will ever be rich, but we all set our own priorities. Are yours in line with your beliefs?

Father, help us handle our finances according to Your wishes, for You are our ultimate authority.

GODLY LIVING

The aged women likewise,
that they be in behaviour as
becometh holiness, not false accusers,
not given to much wine,
teachers of good things.

TITUS 2:3 KJV

Men are not the only ones told to serve as examples of godly living. Women have strengths of their own—such wonderful resources as compassion, fidelity, and love—that need to be taught to the next generation. Because of their role as mother, many women shy away from directly teaching but instead teach through their actions in the church and community. Their seemingly tireless dedication to others is enough to show the depth of their faith and encourages others to pitch in with them.

Whether they organize church fairs, bake a pie for the bake sale, or single-handedly keep the Sunday school running, women have much to teach the community.

Father, I have no great talent to share, but I do have time to invest.
Show me where I am needed the most.

ALWAYS HOPE

*For the needy shall not
alway be forgotten:
the expectation of the poor
shall not perish for ever.*

PSALM 9:18 KJV

The Jewish people end their Passover feast with the words, "Next year in Jerusalem." Every year, through pogroms, persecutions, and horrors of all kinds, Jews around the world have held onto the hope of celebrating their next Passover in Jerusalem. They know, more than most, that "the expectation of the poor shall not perish for ever."

A Christian couple must be able to sustain the same level of hope in their lives, no matter what their current situation. It's not easy when you're playing Russian roulette with the monthly bills or have to send a brilliant child to a trade school instead of the university he or she deserves. But there is always hope.

Father, we know You can work things out for us. In the meantime, give us hope.

TRUE RICHES

There is that maketh himself rich,
yet hath nothing:
there is that maketh himself poor,
yet hath great riches.

PROVERBS 13:7 KJV

What do you consider riches? That's the question every couple has to answer for themselves. Would you lose your spouse and children for the sake of your bank balance, or would you give every penny to keep them with you? If paying your tithe means not paying off your credit card bill, which do you choose? If hiring a tutor to get a child through physics means no vacation, what is your pleasure?

Decisions like these hammer at us unmercifully, day after day. The big ones are pretty easy to figure out, but some of the little ones are tricky. Dinner out or rice and beans at home? Fix the car's transmission or straighten the child's teeth?

The choice is yours.

Father, every decision we make is important. Help us decide where our true riches are and set our priorities in accordance with Your wishes.

ETERNAL LIFE

*Riches profit
not in the day of wrath:
but righteousness
delivereth from death.*

PROVERBS 11:4 KJV

There's no bank in heaven, and even if there were, you'd still arrive at the so-called pearly gates empty-handed. God doesn't care how much cash you leave behind. You did what you did with your life, and money is just part of what you did.

The next time you have to make a life decision, take a minute to think about how that decision will affect your future. Riches can't give you eternal life, but Jesus can and will.

Father, thank You for sending Your Son, Jesus, to redeem us from our sins and wash them away.

Solution to All

Ask the LORD for rain
in the springtime;
it is the LORD who
makes the storm clouds.
He gives showers of rain to men,
and plants of the field to everyone.

ZECHARIAH 10:1 NIV

Both of you may work full-time outside the home, or one may work full-time while the other cares for the house and family, but no matter what your working arrangement, your wealth and security don't come from an employer. Likewise, if you own your own business, you shouldn't pin your hopes on this year's profit.

No business has the answers to every problem. Indeed, no employer can promise happiness, rid you of incurable illness, or provide rain in the midst of a drought. Money can only solve so much. It's a helpful tool but not a god.

God provides all the solutions for our lives, whether it's rain to bring relief to a parched land or arid, clear days that dry out a wet home. He heals unhappy relationships and can cure illnesses doctors can't even identify.

All we have to do is ask and trust in Him.

Our trust is in You, Jesus, not our jobs or businesses. Thank You for providing for our every need.

LIGHT OF SCRIPTURE

*Thy word is
a lamp unto my feet,
and a light unto my path.*

PSALM 119:105 KJV

God's Word lights your path and shows you the way to go. Not reading God's Word is like taking a candle into the dark without lighting the wick. You'll stumble over anything in the road.

Have you read through the whole Bible together? If not, you risk bumbling around spiritually and stubbing your toes on obstacles Satan throws in your way. Your shared light may burn dimly or even nearly go out.

Don't read Scripture on anyone else's time schedule; rather, make it a natural part of your day together. Whether you open the Book together before you start your day or cuddle up in bed with it before you turn out the light, read it.

Once you've finished, start again. After all, just because you used a lamp to light your way one night doesn't mean you can see in the dark. And the light of Scripture burns brighter all the time, as you stow it away in your heart and live by its glow.

Thank You, Lord, for the brightness of Your Word. Let it shine out to others as we read and share it day by day.

FOLLOW THROUGH

But be doers of the word,
not hearers only,
deceiving yourselves.

JAMES 1:22 NKJV

Suppose you walked down the aisle with a member of the opposite sex, spoke the words that made you man and wife, and never lived with that person. How many people would believe you had a real, close relationship?

We wouldn't think of doing such a thing to a person, but many of us do just that to God. We walk down an aisle, claim His Name, but live as if we have no obligations.

Not doing what God calls you to do is like a marriage without commitment: It's not much of a relationship. Because you never followed through on the words you spoke at the altar, you'd find it hard to explain to others that you really loved your spouse. Similarly, commit yourself to Christ and fail to do what He says, and even non-Christians will easily spot your lack of devotion.

If you really love God, don't only read His Word—follow through on it, too. Then the world will know you're committed, and you won't deceive anyone—least of all yourself.

Lord, teach us not to deceive ourselves but to love You with all our hearts and have a complete commitment to acting out Your Word.

Keep Your Promises

I cried unto thee; save me,
and I shall keep thy testimonies.

Psalm 119:146 KJV

Life's crushing us. We didn't follow God's Word because the solution seemed so obvious. With only the best of intentions, we wandered off His path. Now stuck in a swamp of sin, we desperately need help.

We call out, "We'll be good, God. We promise. Just get us out of this!" And for those few seconds we mean it.

Crying out to God and admitting our sin are the right actions to take. As we feel ourselves slipping out of the swamp, His strong arms lifting us out of the muck, we know God keeps His promises. Soon God sets us back on course. He's kept His promises.

Unless we want to be more firmly stuck in that swamp, we must remember that mistake and keep our desperate promise, not forgetting it like some greedy child.

God's testimonies don't change. If we want to be like Him, ours shouldn't either.

Thank You, Father, for saving us from our own well-meaning efforts. Cleanse us from sin today and keep us faithful to Your testimonies.

God's Truth

My lips shall utter praise,
when thou hast taught me
thy statutes.

Psalm 119:171 kjv

O h, no, Bible study again. Instead of looking forward to it, we find Bible reading has become a chore.

Learning God's truths isn't meant to be spiritual drudgery, even when it's hard work. After all, we aren't aiming to start a marital competition to see who can memorize the most Bible verses! Knowing God's statutes should simply bring us to such appreciation of His nature that we burst into praise.

Stilted, worn-out phrases aren't praise, and anyone who tries to praise God that way misses the point: God's wonderful character has so blessed us that we can't stop talking about it. He has saved us, when once we had no care for Him or His truths; He has cleansed us of every sin and trusted us to share His truths with others in our families, workplaces, and world.

That kind of blessing rightly overflows from our lives, in all we say and do.

Lord, thank You for showing us Your love through your Word. Let it overflow into our world through our praise.

FRIEND AND MASTER

"But you, Israel, are My servant,
Jacob, whom I have chosen,
the descendants of Abraham
My friend."

ISAIAH 41:8 NKJV

Sometimes you "just know" what your spouse will think on a subject. He'll pass on an appetizer of mushrooms but never jumbo shrimp. She'll choose a vacation at the shore over one at the mountains.

You know what your mate feels and thinks because you've spent time together and discussed each other's likes and dislikes. You've become friends.

But do you "just know" what your friend Jesus likes and dislikes? Have you spent enough time with Him, through prayer and Bible reading, to have His opinion on the large and small events in life?

If not, you're acting like a servant, not a friend. You haven't drawn close enough to the Master to know that He offers you more than a job. He offers a relationship with Himself that beats any on earth.

Don't turn down that once-in-a-lifetime chance to cultivate an eternal relationship. Who would be servant to a Master who wants to be a Friend?

Jesus, our eternal friendship starts here on earth. We offer You our service and our hearts.

OUR FRIEND JESUS

A man of many companions
may come to ruin,
but there is a friend who
sticks closer than a brother.

PROVERBS 18:24 NIV

B efore you knew Christ, you might have had lots of friends
—or very few. But if you chose your friends because they'd
look good to the world, you were almost certainly disappointed. When you needed someone to help you, that help
was probably scarce.

Christian friendships aren't a head count. No one, least of
all God, judges people by the number of friends they have or
don't have. God isn't in the counting business, and we
shouldn't be either.

God's goal for friendships is depth, not number. A few
close friendships—with other couples or singles—will support
you in trouble when a multitude will fail you. One friend who
stands with you is worth twenty who "just don't have time."

Whether you're giving to a friend or on the receiving end
of help, the model you want to follow isn't what the world
will think, but Jesus.

When it comes to friends, Jesus is the best one ever.

Lord Jesus, help us to model all our friendships on You, especially the
one that makes up our marriage.

LOVING FRIENDSHIPS

Jonathan said to David,
"Go in peace, for we have sworn
friendship with each other
in the name of the LORD, saying,
'The LORD is witness between you and me,
and between your descendants
and my descendants forever.'"

1 SAMUEL 20:42 NIV

Would you rethink your friendships if you knew God were a witness between you?

Jonathan and David knew God was a third party to their friendship. So when Jonathan's father, King Saul, turned against his friend, Israel's prince helped David escape even though he knew he could face his father's wrath.

When David became king, after his friend's death, Jonathan's son Mephibosheth might have been seen as an heir to Saul's throne. Yet David restored Saul's lands to Mephibosheth and honored him with a place at the new king's table (2 Samuel 9). It was not part of David's plan to eradicate his friend's family, as many new rulers would have done.

David's and Jonathan's relationship was not a convenient one that simply filled selfish needs. Can you and your spouse say the same of your friendships?

Lord, we want You to be a witness between us and our friends.
May our friendships reflect Your love.

IMPORTANT WORDS

Wounds from a friend
can be trusted,
but an enemy multiplies kisses.

PROVERBS 27:6 NIV

How could the person you love most say that about you? You thought your spouse was your best friend and now you wonder where that faithful friendship went. Wouldn't anyone rather have kisses than correction?

Criticism from a mate is usually not pleasant. After all, you value this person's opinion over all others. You want to please her or make him admire you.

But you know you're not perfect. None of us is. We all need to make personal changes, and it's a sign of love, not hate, for someone to kindly point out a midcourse correction that could keep your ship from being stranded on the rocks.

The person who just keeps kissing you and never says a word is your real enemy. Don't let the first sign of his or her true feelings be the grinding of rock on your keel.

Lord, help us to be kind and gentle when we point out each other's weaknesses, but help us to say the words that need to be spoken for the good of our marriage.

A Deeper Love

*You adulterous people, don't you know
that friendship with the world is hatred toward God?
Anyone who chooses to be a friend of the world
becomes an enemy of God.*

James 4:4 NIV

Perhaps you cannot imagine being unfaithful to your spouse. You would never hurt one who loves you and does so much for you.

But do you find it equally hard to think of hurting the One who loves you even more than your spouse? Is it easy to hurt God and not feel pain?

Your husband or wife shares a special, profound love with you, but God loves you even more deeply. No one else can take your place with Him, no matter how many people He saves. James compares turning away from His love with adultery.

Turning away from God and to the world separates you from Him as surely as turning to another member of the opposite sex parts you from your mate.

Today, choose whom you'll love: Jesus or the world.

Lord, You've shown us so much love, yet how easily we turn from You. Keep our hearts near You and part us from the world's temptations.

SPACE

Oh, that I had in the desert
a lodging place for travelers,
so that I might leave my people
and go away from them;
for they are all adulterers,
a crowd of unfaithful people.

JEREMIAH 9:2 NIV

Have you ever wanted to run away from home? When daily pressures lean on you, solitude seems most appealing.

The prophet Jeremiah knew how you feel. He wanted to run away from his "job" of telling the people how far they were from God and visit a desert resort.

Every marriage has moments when each member needs some space. An hour or two might help, if you need to think out some things. Or maybe you're tired and need some serious nap time. But don't make that a long parting or you'll risk increasing the emotional distance between you.

Though Jeremiah was irritated and even disgusted by his people, he didn't give up on them. One word from the Lord and he was on the spot again.

Take a break, but don't break with God or your spouse.

Lord, when we need space, help us to be gracious about it and return to each other refreshed.

PERFECT TIMING

"I went out full,
but the LORD has
brought me back empty."

RUTH 1:21 NASB

Naomi had reason to grieve. Her husband and sons had died in Moab, and now Naomi was alone, except for Ruth, one of her daughters-in-law, who refused to forsake her and had accompanied her to Judah. Naomi's lot certainly seemed hard and hopeless. She was right when she said she'd gone out full and come home empty.

But God had blessed Naomi in ways she couldn't imagine. Ruth would be part of the "solution" to make Naomi full again. Through one faithful woman, Naomi would experience the birth of her grandson, Obed. Again, she would feel blessed.

Have you gone out full and come back empty? Perhaps you've made unwise decisions that are affecting your marriage. Maybe you've fallen into sin and are working your way out of its results. You've turned to God for help, but rescue hasn't been quick in coming.

Don't fall prey to bitterness. God isn't finished with your life yet. In His perfect timing, you'll go out full again.

Lord, we know Your filling. Today, whether we are full or empty, we trust in You.

GLORIFY HIM

With praise and thanksgiving
they sang to the LORD: "He is good;
his love to Israel endures forever."
And all the people gave a great shout
of praise to the LORD, because
the foundation of the house
of the LORD was laid.

EZRA 3:11 NIV

As the Israelites began rebuilding their temple, they had an easy time praising God. Joy came naturally as they saw His hand at work.

Thanking God and telling of His wonders is a snap when you're on a spiritual high. But every Christian couple has times when it's hard to see God's "kingdom building" in their lives. Perhaps a loved one dies, or the ministry that started so prosperously faces rough patches. Suddenly praise becomes difficult.

Is the same God who told the Israelites to build the temple still in control of the universe? Is He still good? Or has one of your life circumstances changed His nature?

God does not change; God always deserves praise. Today give Him your richest sacrifice as you glorify Him, despite life's challenges.

No matter what challenges we face today, Jesus, You are still the mighty Lord of our lives. We delight in Your grace and love.

TOTAL DEVOTION TO GOD

Nevertheless, each national group made its own gods
in the several towns where they settled,
and set them up in the shrines the people
of Samaria had made at the high places.

2 KINGS 17:29 NIV

Sargon, the king of Assyria, sent people of many nations to resettle Samaria. When lions began to attack them, he sent a priest along. The pagan king figured Samaria's deity was angry and needed placating.

But the new Samaritans would never really understand Yahweh or what He required. They had toted along their own idols, set up shrines, and worshiped them, along with Yahweh. They imagined that no one would be offended and that everyone could be happy.

Instead they ended up with a religious mess and found themselves despised by faithful Jews and spiritually empty.

Although we don't set figurines up in our homes and bow down to them, we may become idol worshipers in more sophisticated ways. We placate unbelievers instead of sharing our faith. We accept non-Christian practices without a blink of the eye. Suddenly we're in a mess, and we wonder how we got there.

Maybe we slid down the path to Samaria.

Lord, we don't want to live in unfaithfulness. Make our hearts and lips devoted to You.

FREEDOM FROM DARKNESS

The LORD has anointed me
to preach good news to the poor.
He has sent me to bind up
the brokenhearted,
to proclaim freedom for
the captives and release from
darkness for the prisoners.

ISAIAH 61:1 NIV

The Israelites had seen their lives destroyed by a foreign, pagan people before they were carried off as slaves to Babylon. Now God's people were poor in heart and spirit, as well as financially. For them, good news didn't seem to exist.

God didn't rush in and change the circumstances for His disobedient people. But they wouldn't always be broken-hearted captives, sitting in darkness. God promised that some-day He would free them, not just from physical bondage but from sin that had caused this situation in the first place.

We may not be chained slaves, dragged to a foreign land, but we feel the weight of spiritual and emotional chains in our marriage. Today God still offers us freedom and release from darkness.

Have you walked out into the light of His Good News?

Lord Jesus, thank You for freeing us from sin. When its chains seek to wrap around us, we turn to You to break their strength.

STAND FIRM

I will heal their backsliding,
I will love them freely:
for mine anger is
turned away from him.

HOSEA 14:4 KJV

How easy to slide into sin, and how hard to break away from it!

Turning away from sin means a serious fight against temptation. You grasp your spiritual weapons and charge into the fray. But just when you feel you've made real headway, you run smack against the same sin. Is God angry with you? Will you ever have victory?

God may let you fight sin for a while. Perhaps you need to learn its cost, so you'll evade it another time. But keep on avoiding that sin, fighting back with God's Word, and seeking to do right, and it will become a thing of the past.

The pain of separation from God felt so sharp when you disobeyed Him. God felt angry and distant. But as you waged battle, you began to understand how much He hated the sin that kept you from Him. You felt His love return.

As His healing filled your being, you stood firm against temptation. You slid back where you should be.

Thank You, Lord, for keeping us from sin. Turn us from it each day so we may rejoice in Your love.

FREEDOM

"If you continue in My word,
then you are truly disciples of Mine;
and you will know the truth,
and the truth will make you free."

JOHN 8:31–32 NASB

Jesus makes us truly free. When we first believe in Him, we may feel swept clean of sin. How wonderful it is to have all the cobwebs dusted from our spirits!

But if we follow that new life with wrong deeds, those cobwebs pile up again, and we're more aware of them than ever. Now we really know what grungy feels like.

Jesus frees us from sin, but we don't stay liberated long if we ignore the truths of His Word. He didn't provide us with a new lifestyle to have us slip back into wrongdoing. Instead, He gave us specific ways to avoid sin.

True disciples don't try to see how much sin they can "get away with." They know God freed them for a purpose, and it wasn't to see how far they could go.

Lord Jesus, thank You for providing us with such freedom. We want to obey Your Word and fulfill Your purpose for our lives.

Walk with God

*But now having been
freed from sin and
enslaved to God,
you derive your benefit,
resulting in sanctification,
and the outcome, eternal life.*

Romans 6:22 nasb

L oosed from sin, you become not a free agent, who runs his or her own life, but a slave of God. There is no third option; you serve God or Satan.

Slavery to God is nothing like slavery to sin. Where once you did wrong, no matter how hard you struggled, now you do right, though not perfectly. Every day you become more and more like Jesus. Instead of bondage, freedom from sin rules your soul, and love replaces hatred in your heart. That can't help but improve your marriage.

You may not be a perfect mate, but if you walk closely with God, as you become more like Him, you'll be more caring and forgiving. Both you and your spouse will see faith's benefits.

Yet God has even more in store for you—eternal life together with Him.

Such freedom as You offer, Lord, cannot be found in sin. Thank You for making us free in all things.

THE GREATEST GIFT

For the wages of sin is death,
but the free gift of God is
eternal life in Christ Jesus our Lord.

ROMANS 6:23 NASB

All we could earn, out of our own efforts, was death. Hard as we tried, nothing could clean us up enough to approach the Holy One. Seeing our filthy, disgusting rags, who could blame Him for excluding us from His holy heaven?

We had it all wrong, though. Earning brownie points or saving up enough good deeds wouldn't get us into heaven. God had a free gift prepared for us, one He wanted to place in our hands. But we turned away.

God shows us what free is really like by giving a lavish gift we could never hope to afford. But He doesn't stop there. This gift is not only valuable for this life alone but also draws us into never-ending days, shared with Him.

All this, simply for opening our arms and hearts to accept the greatest gift available in time or eternity: Jesus.

We open our arms to You each day, Jesus. Give us freedom to share Your gift with the world.

CHILDREN

But it is the spirit in a man,
the breath of the Almighty,
that gives him understanding.
It is not only the old who are wise,
not only the aged who
understand what is right.

JOB 32:8–9 NIV

We spend years teaching our children, correcting them, and, oh yes, worrying about them (a hard habit to break). Then one day they surprise us and grow into wonderful, capable adults.

Of course a good part of this comes from the way we raised them, and this should give us joy. But much of their wisdom comes from within themselves, from their spirit, their own hard-won understanding. Don't feel unneeded or abandoned when your children show unexpected maturity. Rejoice!

Father, give our children Your guidance throughout their lives. We cannot raise them properly on our own. We need Your help.

Good Deeds

"Take heed that you do not do
your charitable deeds before men,
to be seen by them.
Otherwise you have no reward
from your Father in heaven."

Matthew 6:1 NKJV

When we do a good deed, it's very hard to keep it to ourselves. Part of that is because we often surprise ourselves. We let an elderly person go ahead of us at the supermarket, then mentally ask, "Wow, where did that come from?" Our reward may be a smile, or it may be nothing more than a warm internal feeling.

Random acts of kindness are never planned and seldom rewarded by those around us at the time. They are secrets between two people and God. But God remembers them, and they will be rewarded.

Father, we may or may not have the means to give generously to charity, but we all have the ability to give of ourselves. When we do, help us not to seek or expect the praise of others. You see. That's enough.

HOPE FOR CHILDREN

All your children shall be
taught by the LORD,
and great shall be
the peace of your children.

ISAIAH 54:13 NKJV

We can prepare our children for life on their own, but the best thing we can do for them is to introduce them to the Lord. He is the only One who can give them peace.

What is the greatest hope you have for your children? Isn't it that, no matter what they become or accomplish, they should be happy? How can you teach them that? Your children may be rich or poor, famous or humble, but only God's peace will bring them true happiness.

Father, only You and Your lessons can give our children the happiness we want for them. We do the best we can for them and trust the rest to You.

The Never Changing One

For You are my hope,
O Lord God;
You are my trust from my youth.
By You I have been
upheld from my birth.

Psalm 71:5–6 NKJV

Almost everything we count on in life has the potential of failing us, of letting us down when we need it the most. Love cools, trust is betrayed, hope is lost. Parents can fail us, children can turn against us, friends can become enemies. Eventually, even our own bodies will betray us and fail to function properly.

Only God is eternal and never changing, the One who holds us up and never betrays our trust. Only God gives us hope in our darkest moments when all else has failed.

Lord, in a disappointing, human world, You are our strength, the One we turn to when we are alone and afraid. Thank You for Your constant, abiding love that brightens our lives.

ABSOLUTE MONARCH

*Wives, submit unto
your own husbands,
as unto the Lord.*

EPHESIANS 5:22 KJV

I am the ruler of this house, and we'll do it my way," he said.

"You are the king here," his wife admitted, "but do you know the difference between an absolute monarch and a constitutional one?"

"Ah. . ."

"An absolute monarch holds total authority. His wishes are supreme." She paused. "There aren't many of them around today."

"No?"

She shook her head. "A constitutional monarch rules with the consent of his or her subjects. They give the king his powers, and they can take them away. They can do away with the whole office or make him just a figurehead."

"I get it. I'm a constitutional monarch, but you hold all the real power."

"Yes, your highness," she replied with a smile.

Lord, no matter how we divide the responsibilities between us, You are the absolute monarch of our family, and we seek Your guidance in every matter.

DWELL IN SAFETY

And they shall no more
be a prey to the heathen,
neither shall the beast of
the land devour them;
but they shall dwell safely,
and none shall make them afraid.

EZEKIEL 34:28 KJV

Accounts of natural disasters, be they floods, fires, earthquakes, or hurricanes, are splashed almost daily on front pages around the world. We feel powerless to protect ourselves on so many fronts, knowing the best we can do is react to disasters when they come, not prevent them.

Yet God promises the righteous that they will dwell in safety and even prosper in this dangerous world as a sign of His care and love. Above all, "none shall make them afraid."

Father, we thank You for Your protection in difficult times.
Although we may taste some suffering, You are our strength and
Sustainer.

In Spite of Ourselves

For if our heart condemn us,
God is greater than our heart,
and knoweth all things.

1 John 3:20 kjv

We disappoint ourselves so easily. True, we are sinful beings, but we want to be better, and when we aren't, we suffer the pangs of guilt. This is especially true in our relationships with our spouses, the ones we love so much and often treat so poorly. At the end of a bad day, our husbands or wives bear the brunt of our disappointments and defeats. Why do they put up with us? Because they understand, they know our true hearts, and they love us in spite of ourselves.

Father, when we dump all our troubles on each other, give our partners Your comfort. Help us overcome our guilt for the sake of our love.

CLOSENESS

And it shall come to pass,
that before they call, I will answer;
and while they are yet speaking,
I will hear.

ISAIAH 65:24 KJV

After a few years of marriage, we become so attuned to the other that we find ourselves completing each other's sentences. We anticipate what the other will want, bringing out a snack without being asked or folding the paper to highlight an article we know the other will want to read. We go so far as to turn down invitations we know the other would dread. In many little ways, the two of us have truly become one.

When you are feeling far away from God, remember that He knows and loves you even more than your spouse does. He anticipates your wants and needs, just as your spouse does, and always wants to please you.

Father, thank You for bringing us so close, and remind us that this is just a taste of how You feel for us.

CARE IN OLD AGE

And even to your old age I am he;
and even to hoar hairs will I carry you:
I have made, and I will bear;
even I will carry, and will deliver you.

ISAIAH 46:4 KJV

Old age frightens us. What if we cannot care for ourselves or our spouse? Will we become a burden to our children? Will we outlive our savings? Who will love us when we turn into irritable old men and sharp-tongued old women?

God promises that He will care for us in our old age, even if others fail us. If necessary, He will pick us up and carry us, for He made us and loves us and will always take care of us.

Father, thank You for this promise that gives us comfort as our hair turns gray and our strength fades. Getting old can be a burden, but You will always support us.

UPS AND DOWNS

Weeping may endure for a night,
but joy cometh in the morning.

PSALM 30:5 KJV

Relationships have their ups and downs. A thoughtless comment, the wrong tone of voice, or even a look can wound us. But when tempers cool and reason returns, the disagreement usually proves to have been a waste of precious time and emotion.

The same thing happens in our relationship with God. We get angry with Him, and He probably gets angry with us, but we both are quick to forgive. It's hard to stay angry with someone who loves you totally, no matter how foolishly you act.

Father, Your forgiveness and the joy it brings us are examples of the way we should treat our partners when we disagree or have our feelings hurt. Remind us of that the next time we feel wounded by the other.

HIS RIGHTEOUSNESS

*For the wrath of man
worketh not the
righteousness of God.*

JAMES 1:20 KJV

As we watch the news or read the newspaper, we may feel our blood pressure start to rise. Accounts of murderers, child molesters, terrorists, and others who hurt innocent people stir us into righteous indignation. We hope the law will deal as harshly with them as they did to others. And if they get away with it, we often wonder where God is.

But God reminds us that our wrath has nothing to do with His righteousness. We could be wrong, but He never is. While He will always understand our wrath, we cannot begin to understand His righteousness.

Father, we know You are there when the innocent suffer, and we trust Your judgment of the evil ones in our midst. Our justice may fail, but Yours will not.

COOL AND COMPOSED

The discretion of a man
deferreth his anger;
and it is his glory to
pass over a transgression.

PROVERBS 19:11 KJV

Some people are unflappable. They remain cool and composed when the rest of us would go into orbit. Are they totally emotionless, unable to love or hate? If you are married to such a person, the temptation is to try to pick a fight now and then, just to see if anything rattles your spouse.

Yet the Bible tells us that discreet people do have emotions and do get angry. Yet they "pass over" the transgressions of others, much as God does with ours, and this is to their glory. Trying to pick a fight with such people will not work. They will feel hurt, and then they will forgive you—which will only drive you crazy.

Lord, we are two very different people who react differently to anger and pain. Give us understanding and patience with each other.

KNOW-IT-ALL

Seest thou a man wise
in his own conceit?
there is more hope of a fool
than of him.

PROVERBS 26:12 KJV

We all know people who believe they know everything. A question comes up, they state the answer, and that's that. They don't even have to think about a problem to be right in their own eyes. In that lies their downfall, because a fool who takes time to think about a problem will come up with a better solution than someone who believes he has all the answers.

If you are married to one of these people, your patience will be sorely tested. You may have a wonderful, loving spouse, but sometimes you'll want to shake him or her and yell, "Think about it, will you?" Sometimes, because that person loves you, he or she will.

Lord, we know that only You are right all the time, but we have too much faith in ourselves. At such times, have patience with us and gently show us where we are wrong so we may follow Your guidance in our lives.

LISTENING

*Listen, for I have
worthy things to say;
I open my lips to speak
what is right.*

PROVERBS 8:6 NIV

Conversation reveals the inner person. When we're dating, we absorb every word our date utters and file each precious comment away for future reference. Some of our dates disqualify themselves the moment they open their mouths, but then we find the right one and marry, largely because of what that person said.

A few years later, we stop listening. We know our spouse so well that his or her comments are predictable, and we've heard them all before. We stop talking about hopes and dreams and beliefs and limit our conversation to the weather, work, and children.

It doesn't have to be this way. Listen to your spouse with as much attention and affection as you listened while you were dating, and you may find your love is deeper than you ever imagined.

Lord, remind us of those long conversations we used to have and how they helped our love to grow. We still have much to learn about each other, if we will only listen.

In God's Hands

*For God is not
a God of disorder
but of peace.*

1 Corinthians 14:33 NIV

L ife is not neat. It's full of disorder, loose ends, and unre-
solved conflicts that keep us from feeling at peace.
There's no point at which we can clap our hands and say,
"There! The children are grown. That part of our life is over."

In the same vein, we can never say, "We have overcome
all our faults. We're perfect now," or "We have all we need
saved up for retirement." As humans, we will never be free of
disorder. God, however, brings order out of chaos. He knows
how all our stories end and is happy to point out the way we
should go.

The next time you are overwhelmed by life's disorder,
place it all in God's hand and taste His peace.

*Father, life can be so confusing when we rely on our own actions.
Help us turn our problems over to You, the only source of true peace
and order.*

LOVE AND HONOR

Jesus said to them,
"Only in his hometown,
among his relatives and
in his own house is
a prophet without honor."

MARK 6:4 NIV

Have you ever been to an awards banquet and heard your spouse praised to the skies by people you don't even know? It doesn't take long before you wonder who these people are talking about.

His successful planning lifted a company out of financial disaster? He can't even balance the family checkbook! Her insightful article brought positive public relations to the firm? They should see the inside of her medicine cabinet! Who is this person you live with?

It's hard to honor someone when you intimately know his or her every fault, but it's foolish to laugh when your spouse is praised by others. Smile proudly, accept their compliments at face value, and honor the one you love.

Father, we don't know each other as well as we think, and we seldom give each other deserved credit. Make us proud of our spouse's achievements because they honor us, too.

FORGET THE REST

Remember ye not the former things,
neither consider the things of old.

ISAIAH 43:18 KJV

We all go into marriage with twenty or thirty years of baggage, a good part of which is dirty laundry. We have a past, and not all of it was pretty. Most of this will come out during courtship, but not all.

While there will still be unconfessed episodes in every couple's past life, marriage is a new start, and no one should let the burdens of the past hang over the present. Confess what you can and forget the rest. God forgives your sins, so give them up and enjoy your new life as a couple.

Father, even when we confess our sins to You and receive Your for-giveness, we may not be able to confess them to each other. Don't let the past ruin our present. Help us accept Your forgiveness and be at peace with our past.

BEST FRIENDS

*Do not
forsake your friend.*

PROVERBS 27:10 NIV

When the kids are grown and gone, leaving the two of you to rattle around the house alone, you may make the astounding discovery that your best friend is your own spouse. You will still have other friends, but your best friend will be the one with whom you've shared most of a lifetime.

Such a discovery usually comes as a surprise. The passion of youth may have faded, and you've certainly had your share of arguments and disagreements, but the one you trust and love the most is still the same. What a joy to grow old with your best friend!

Father, thank You for all You have given us as a couple, especially for the deep, abiding friendship we still share after all these years.

EVERYDAY LOVE

And Jacob loved Rachel; and said,
I will serve thee seven years
for Rachel thy younger daughter.

GENESIS 29:18 KJV

Young people think it's romantic the way Jacob gave up seven years of his life for Rachel. Such sacrifice and devotion! They never stop to think that once the seven years were over, Jacob signed up for a lifetime of service to Rachel, binding himself to love her, protect her, and help her raise the children. Compared to that, the seven years were a snap.

Romance is wonderful, but reality is even more so. The next time you feel that love has grown cold in your marriage, remember all the daily sacrifices your spouse has made for the sake of the family. Hanging in there for all those years is far more romantic than seven years of waiting.

Lord, remind us that true love is shown in the daily business of living. It may not be romantic, but it brings us together and shows us exactly what You mean love to be: service to others.

Love Your Neighbor

A man who lacks judgment
derides his neighbor,
but a man of understanding
holds his tongue.

Proverbs 11:12 NIV

Couples usually see more of their neighbors than they do their relatives. That's good, as neighbors are likely to be more helpful than relatives in a crisis, simply because they're closer. You might not choose your neighbors as friends—you sort of work with what you have—but you do have much in common with them and would do well to keep neighborly relations polite and friendly.

One of the best ways of doing this is to never say a bad word about one neighbor to another, no matter what the provocation. Your words will always come back to haunt you. The best advice is still to love your neighbor.

Lord, remind us to treat all our neighbors with respect and use discretion in our conversations with them.

GOD'S BEAUTY

Splendor and majesty are before Him,
strength and beauty are in His sanctuary.

PSALM 96:6 NASB

Y ou may think of your wife as beautiful, but you probably don't often ponder God's beauty.

None of us know what Jesus looked like on earth, yet He
wasn't physically attractive (see Isaiah 53:2). Still, the Psalm-
ist isn't talking about God's face; he's commenting on His
personality.

Perhaps you've known someone who wouldn't win a
beauty contest but had a "great personality." After a while,
you didn't care what that person looked like—you were friends.
God is something like that. Once you know Him, though
you can't see His face, you know His beauty and want more
of Him.

God isn't just a pretty personality. He also has unlimited
splendor, majesty, and strength. The more you look at Him,
the more there is to see.

Have you looked at Him today and seen His strength?
Have you seen His splendor and worshiped His majesty?

Come close to Him today.

Father God, we don't often appreciate Your beauty, strength, splen-
dor, and majesty. Forgive us for our shallowness. We want to know
You better.

GENTLE TRUTH

"And like their bow
they have bent their tongues for lies.
They are not valiant for the truth on the earth.
For they proceed from evil to evil,
and they do not know Me,"
says the LORD.

JEREMIAH 9:3 NKJV

Telling the truth takes courage. People don't like to hear the truth when they're caught up in pleasant but disastrous lies. They'd rather enjoy the fun now and ignore the price they'll pay down the road.

Telling the truth in marriage can be particularly hard. After all, you can't stage a "truth attack" and then walk away. You have to live with your spouse day in and day out.

We all need to understand that ignoring the truth just gets us into deeper trouble. In biblical terms, we go "from evil to evil." Avoiding evil means listening to a truthful spouse, weighing his or her words, and being willing to make changes.

Truth isn't our enemy, and neither is that spouse. A reality check that draws us closer to God may be a spouse's loving gift.

Lord, teach us to speak gentle truth to each other and to know when it has been spoken.

LET YOUR LIGHT SHINE

Your father, the devil. . .was a murderer
from the beginning, not holding to the truth,
for there is no truth in him.
When he lies, he speaks his native language,
for he is a liar and the father of lies.

JOHN 8:44 NIV

The "father of lies," Satan, has fooled many people into believing that marriage is a partnership of misery. Out of fear they shun it, living together instead or completely avoiding relationships.

Satan's lie murders marriage. But how can people whose parents fought and made each other unhappy understand marital happiness? How can they believe in something they've never seen?

Happily married Christians kill Satan's lie by making their marriages witnesses to young people caught in doubt. By sharing time with others, telling them of God's plan for marriage, letting them see marital joy, and providing an example of positive behavior, Christians shine light into lives darkened by Satan's lies.

God's truth begins in the home, with our own families, and beams out into the world.

Lord, we offer our marriage up to You, as a witness to the truth of Your love. We want to show forth the truth of the life You have established.

TRUE COMMITMENT

For when they shall say,
Peace and safety:
then sudden destruction cometh upon them,
as travail upon a woman with child;
and they shall not escape.

1 THESSALONIANS 5:3 KJV

You've heard all the public promises about the goodness of life. "All is fine," politicians say. "You don't have to worry!" But suddenly a disaster strikes, and the emptiness of those words becomes apparent.

Spiritually a day is coming when the emptiness of unfulfilled promises to God will be shown. People who claimed to know Jesus, but don't, will be shocked to discover the everlasting life they could have had, had they made a lasting commitment. Those folks may be family members, friends— or even us.

No one should be fooled by words of safety. None of us can escape spiritually if we are trying to "butter up" God, though our hearts are cold toward Him.

Only in our commitment to Him are we truly safe, and our hearts are the thermometers that show our spiritual temperatures.

How many degrees is your heart registering now?

Whether we're speaking to friends or family, Lord, people need to hear Your offer of love. Fire up our hearts today.

GOD'S VOICE

But as touching brotherly love
ye need not that I write unto you:
for ye yourselves are taught
of God to love one another.

1 THESSALONIANS 4:9 KJV

How can you increase your love for other Christians? Paul doesn't offer "The Twelve Steps of Brotherly Love" or give the Thessalonians any new directions on how to love each other. That lesson comes directly from God.

When it comes to our brothers and sisters in Christ, God shows us ways to love them. We hear of a need here and fill it. We become aggravated at a brother's actions and deal with them gently or let them pass, as God guides us. The Spirit works in our hearts to show what is best.

Only when we ignore His still, small voice do we land ourselves in trouble. Without His guidance, small problems increase and destroy a church. Little sins, constantly fed, become large problems.

Whether that "brother" is your spouse or a Christian from your congregation, listen to God's voice. A few quiet moments with God are worth a thousand steps.

Thank You, Lord, for showing us how to love one another. This day, fill our hearts with ways to express that love.

FEEDING YOUR FAITH

We are bound to thank God always for you, brethren. . .
because that your faith groweth exceedingly,
and the charity of every one of you
all toward each other aboundeth.

2 THESSALONIANS 1:3 KJV

Though they faced great pressure, the Thessalonians had one thing down pat: They knew how to love each other. Persecution and trials hadn't made these Christians turn on each other. If anything, such torments had purified their love.

When we face trials, how do we act? Do we turn to each other for support or head off in opposite directions, saying, "It's all my spouse's fault"?

None of us need to experience a faith persecution to find how we'd respond. We discover our mettle when money becomes tight or a family member is in trouble. Suddenly it can become "my money" versus "your money" or "my family" opposing "yours."

The Thessalonians pleased God—and Paul—by feeding their faith, not dissension. And in the end they blessed themselves by sharing a greater brotherly love. Are you blessing yourselves, too?

We need to love each other and fellow Christians, Lord. Open our hearts to the words of Your Spirit.

SPREADING THE GOSPEL

Finally, brethren,
pray for us. . .that we may be delivered
from unreasonable and wicked men:
for all men have not faith.
But the Lord is faithful.

2 THESSALONIANS 3:1–3 KJV

I t almost goes without saying that not everyone you meet in life will be a Christian. A few nonbelievers will get your goat, drive you nuts, and make you wish you'd never met them. They'll make unreasonable demands or do downright evil things. Perhaps they'll even demand that you act as if you didn't have any faith. Certainly, they don't welcome your witness.

Just because God graced Paul with an amazing set of spiritual gifts didn't keep Paul from running into guys who stood in the way of the spread of the gospel. Paul doesn't sound as if he relished knowing these folks.

Like Paul, we meet people who accept our testimony about God and those who cause us nothing but grief. We thank Him for our "Thessalonians," who eagerly hear more, and we sometimes pray for deliverance from the others.

But whether we thank or pray, we trust in God's faithfulness. After all, that's what spreads the gospel in the end.

When we run into people who don't like our message, Lord, help us
remember that it's Yours, not ours.

GOD'S STRENGTH

But ye, brethren,
be not weary in well doing.

2 THESSALONIANS 3:13 KJV

About time someone told the brethren that, some woman out there is thinking. Women often tend to do a lot of "well doing." Caring for families, taking part in church activities, and facing an overloaded to-do list can make them irritable. After all, how can anyone fit one more task on that mile-long sheet?

But God isn't just speaking to men here; He's talking to all Christians. "Well doing" doesn't mean having the longest to-do list or being on every church board. It means not giving up on doing right: loving that child who is straying, responding to hatred with love, and hanging in there when times are tough.

There will be times when doing right doesn't seem to get its proper payback or when the difficult situation seems stronger than we are. "Do not get weary," Paul says. God will give you strength.

All of us need His strength for just one more day, and one more hour, to hold on all the way.

Give us Your strength, gracious Lord, when we feel tempted to give in. We need Your energy, flowing through us, to complete Your tasks.

OPEN HEARTS

*"When you see the ark
of the covenant of the LORD your God,
and the priests, who are Levites, carrying it,
you are to move out from
your positions and follow it.
Then you will know which way to go,
since you have never been
this way before."*

JOSHUA 3:3–4 NIV

Wouldn't it be great to just look up and see where God is leading you? Lift your eyes and God's ark would show you the way. The Israelites could hardly make a mistake with God so obviously present.

For a short time, all was well. The Israelites crossed the Jordan. But in Joshua 7:7 their leader started questioning why God brought them into the Promised Land. "Are you going to destroy us?" Joshua asked. Discouragement, caused by sin, had obliterated that obvious path.

God doesn't usually lead by putting a physical sign before us. He leads our hearts. When we don't open them to His way, He could drive a Mack truck before us, and we wouldn't see it.

Are your hearts open to Him today?

Lord, we don't need an ark in front of us to see Your will. Open our hearts so we can follow Your path.

SOVEREIGN LORD

And Joshua said, "Ah, Sovereign LORD,
why did you ever bring this people
across the Jordan to deliver us into the
hands of the Amorites to destroy us?
If only we had been content to stay
on the other side of the Jordan!"

JOSHUA 7:7 NIV

S overeign Lord? The words that follow seem to show that
Joshua missed the point entirely. If God is sovereign and
can do what He wills, the leader of the Hebrews could trust
that God had a purpose for bringing them across the Jordan.
A sovereign God was still in control, and Joshua could trust
in Him.

We know what it's like to struggle as Joshua did. We start
on a path, certain of God's direction. At first, all is clear, and life
runs smoothly. Then we hit the first roadblock. "Ah, Sovereign
Lord," we cry, "how did we get ourselves in this mess?"

The ark isn't out in front of us anymore. We have to trust,
and that isn't always easy. But we, too, can look back at the
"Jordans" God has carried us across, the sins He's wiped out
of our lives, and the situations He's brought us through.

No matter what we face, He still is sovereign Lord.

Lord, when it's hard to trust in You, remind us that You are sover-
eign Lord. Reign over our lives.

HOLDING ON TO FAITH

*Now faith is
the assurance of things hoped for,
the conviction of things not seen.*

HEBREWS 11:1 NASB

Faith is for those moments when nothing seems to go right. When you've reached the end of your rope and just can't hold on, and you wish you could live someone else's life—one with no troubles—you need faith.

That's because faith is tied to hope. One doesn't come without the other. When you're stuck in a tough situation, you need to be able to hold on to hope and to see the unseen long enough to know that your situation is not forever.

The author of Hebrews continues by listing many men and women and the benefits of their faith. They didn't physically receive all God's promises any more than we do, but they held on in faith, receiving many benefits in this life and an eternal reward.

When life isn't going perfectly, hold on to your convictions and someday you'll be glorifying God, along with Abel, Enoch, Noah, Abraham, Sarah. . .

Following so great a cloud of witnesses who trusted in You, we need not doubt, O Lord.

FOCUS ON JESUS

Therefore,
since we have so great a cloud
of witnesses surrounding us,
let us also lay aside every encumbrance. . .
fixing our eyes on Jesus,
the author and perfecter of faith.

HEBREWS 12:1–2 NASB

Okay, your faith isn't perfect. There are days when doubt and trouble get you down. Abraham and Sarah had them, too. But they kept their eyes in the right place, and those imperfect days didn't destroy them.

We don't perfect our faith. It's not a matter of getting every spiritual jot and tittle right and making a daily exhibition of massive self-control. If we micromanaged our lives like that, we'd never become perfect. We'd end up being legalistic instead.

But when we focus on Jesus, changes happen in our lives. While we're not even looking—because we have our eyes on Him—we start experiencing an unexpected fruit of the Spirit. We were obeying Him in one place, and He gave us an unanticipated gift.

We're just focusing on the Master, along with that great cloud of witnesses who have gone before us.

We want to keep our eyes on You, Lord. Keep our vision fixed there.

OVERCOMING

For whatsoever is born of God
overcometh the world: and this is the victory that
overcometh the world, even our faith.
Who is he that overcometh the world,
but he that believeth that Jesus is
the Son of God?

1 JOHN 5:4–5 KJV

O vercoming sounds hard, doesn't it? Climbing a mountain or fighting off an enemy might make an appropriate word picture, but faith in Jesus? That somehow seems too simple. Faith seems too lightweight a concept to overcome anything.

But our mistaken preconceptions won't do here. John isn't talking about a touchy-feely faith that's strong one day and weak the next. He's talking about the Christian who takes risks for his faith or suffers for her beliefs.

Overcoming the world isn't a piece of cake. It takes great effort to do the right thing when wrong is so tempting. Doing God's will, when the world says it's silly, challenges us.

Those struggles we go through aren't meaningless, though they may seem so at the time. They're really indicators of overcoming.

Are both of you overcoming today?

Lord, when we face struggles, help us to see them as indicators that we're overcoming the world—for You.

CONFIDENT IN GOD'S CARE

The righteous cry out,
and the LORD hears them;
he delivers them from
all their troubles.

PSALM 34:17 NIV

When faith seems difficult, we struggle to understand its privileges. Trials conceal the truth concerning the benefits that come with being God's child.

Unbelief obscures the tender care He has for His children. After all, nonbelievers would find it hard to believe that God cared much for their greatest problems, much less the intimate details of their day. Only with faith comes the certainty of love.

As God's children, you can be confident He cares for every trouble, even the small, irritating ones that still ruin a day in seconds.

Face the loss of a loved one or a minor argument with the same confidence: God cares for your troubles. Cry out softly or shout it from the rooftops, and He will hear.

Lord, You have shown Your love in so many ways, yet we still miss the point. Thank You for the privilege of coming to You with even our small irritations.

Never Lose Hope

So he gave them his attention,
expecting to receive something from them.
Then Peter said,
". . .What I do have I give you:
In the name of Jesus Christ of Nazareth,
rise up and walk."

Acts 3:5–6 NKJV

That morning when the lame man came to the gate, perhaps he'd mumbled a prayer for help, but doubtless he
hadn't expected much of an answer. A few coins were all he
wanted. Not much to ask for, was it, God? After all, everyone has to live.

Hope didn't have a chance in his heart. Two men who
didn't have a penny on them approached. One spoke, and the
beggar no longer needed to beg. Where once hope had died,
it rose expectantly.

Feeling hopeless today? Jesus still makes life changes in
people who don't expect them. He comes to those who are
far from Him and calls their names. Suddenly, like the lame
man, they're whole and hopeful.

Have you turned to the One who heals beggars? All you
have to do is ask.

Lord, our expectations are often so much smaller than Yours. Light
hope in our hearts.

CONSTANT LOVE

A friend loves at all times,
and a brother is born
for adversity.

PROVERBS 17:17 NKJV

"Marry your best friend" is not bad advice, but that best friend you marry is still different from you. You do dishes right after supper, when he isn't ready. He does things at lightning speed, when you prefer a slower pace.

Minor marital differences can work for or against you, depending on how you deal with them. Turn each one into a fight and your relationship becomes a battleground. Recognize them for what they are—differences that aren't the end of the world—and peace reigns again.

Small issues that act like sand in the gears of your marriage don't have to ruin your relationship. God never said two people had to agree constantly, but they do have to love at all times and stick with each other through the trials. After all, if your spouse is a Christian, you married a brother or sister in the faith.

Treat your spouse with constant love, and you'll develop a great friendship—and a terrific romance.

Thank You, Lord, for the friendship You've given us. Help us not to let the sand get in the gears of our marriage.

GOD IS IN CONTROL

"Even if Babylon reaches the sky
and fortifies her lofty stronghold,
I will send destroyers against her,"
declares the LORD.

JEREMIAH 51:53 NIV

One day life can seem good. Things are going your way, and God seems to be "on your side." The next day disaster strikes, and you're left looking miserable, while those awful sinners across the street or across town have a picture-perfect life.

"Why me, Lord?" you may cry. "Didn't I try to obey You? What went wrong?" You may be tempted to look at Mr. and Mrs. Sinner with a jaundiced eye and wonder why they aren't in your shoes instead.

You don't need to begin evening up the "score." God still has everything under control, both in your life and your neighbor's. Those who ignore God may have a reprieve during this lifetime—or they may have a world of silent misery inside—but God deals with them in His own time. It's not ours to judge and condemn.

When our trials come, whys or bitterness bring us nothing. Trusting that God is in control holds the real answer.

We may never know why, but we know the One who holds "Why?"
in His hands—You.

Turn to God

Jezebel his wife said,
"Is this how you act as king over Israel?
Get up and eat! Cheer up.
I'll get you the vineyard
of Naboth the Jezreelite."

1 KINGS 21:7 NIV

Need help? Ask your wife or husband—unless you're King Ahab, that is. Help like Jezebel's a spouse doesn't need.

When Ahab wanted a vineyard and Naboth wouldn't sell his property, which was his inheritance, the king went home to sulk. But the king's wife, that tough cookie Jezebel, had a plan to fix everything: Kill Naboth and take his land for yourself.

The tough cookies of this world often have it tough. They try harder and harder to make life go where they want, and things never seem to work out. That's because they're looking for vineyards when they should be looking to God. They're hoping this world will come up with answers that belong to the Almighty.

Want to help your spouse? Don't be a tough cookie—turn to God instead.

Lord, when we need help, we know where to go for it. You have every answer to our needs. We turn to You today.

APPRECIATION

Now the people complained about their hardships
in the hearing of the LORD, and when he heard them
his anger was aroused.

NUMBERS 11:1 NIV

Complaints quickly get hard to take. Mention something once and your spouse probably won't mind. Perhaps a second time will be okay, too, but once or twice more, and you'll end up with a marital squabble.

God didn't appreciate complaints from His people either. "Traveling all this way in the desert is a pain," some probably said. "It makes our feet sore." "We don't like the food!" objected others. Dissatisfaction rang in His ears instead of the praises that should have been there. The Holy One became angry.

The complaints of His people showed they didn't really appreciate Him and His salvation from Egypt. He'd tried to lead them into the Promised Land, but they'd objected. That sin of disobedience had landed them in the desert.

Don't turn your marriage into a desert of complaints. Instead, appreciate your spouse. You'll diffuse anger—and avoid sore feet!

We know we need to keep our complaints to a minimum, Lord.
Show us instead how to appreciate You and that special spouse.

Sweeping Sin Away

David burned with anger
against the man and said to Nathan,
"As surely as the LORD lives,
the man who did this
deserves to die!"

2 SAMUEL 12:5 NIV

When David passed judgment on the wealthy man whom he thought had stolen another's only lamb, death seemed a just punishment. The king didn't know that the prophet who told him the tale was pointing out the monarch's own sin. David had stolen the only wife of Uriah the Hittite, committing adultery with her, and Nathan rebuked him through that story.

Until then, David thought he'd sinned without being caught. Thinking no one except he and Bathsheba knew, David forgot about God or thought He'd ignored that trespass.

We, too, think we "get away" with sin. God doesn't press us about a wrongdoing, so we think it's okay. But suddenly we find we've underestimated Him. What we've swept under the carpet trips us up again.

In your marriage are you tripping over sins? Bring them to God so He can sweep the bad out of your lives.

Sweep sin out of our lives, Lord God. We don't want anything to keep us from loving You.

REVERENCE FOR THE WORD

" 'Why did you despise
the word of the LORD
by doing what is
evil in his eyes?' "

2 SAMUEL 12:9 NIV

Have you ever despised the Word of the Lord? *We wouldn't do that,* you may think. *A hallmark of believing Christians is love for God's Word: We love what God says because we love Him and want to obey Him.*

But if we really love God, we not only revere His Word, we obey it. When He declares something is wrong, we don't figure we'll do it "just this once." Sin doesn't slip into our lives as it did into David's.

We also don't want to use God's Word without compassion. For some, Scripture becomes a weapon to wound other believers who don't accept their legalistic interpretation. Their harsh adherence to man-made rules is not of God.

Take the Word seriously. God does. When Christians ignore or misuse it, He takes it very personally. Despise His Word, and you despise the One who gave it to you.

Lord, we love You and Your Word. Help us to obey You today.

KNOWLEDGE

For in much wisdom
is much grief,
and he who increases
knowledge increases sorrow.

ECCLESIASTES 1:18 NKJV

There's so much in the world that we wish we didn't know, so much that we hope our children will never learn through sad experience. War and famine come right into our living rooms after dinner with the early news, and the eleven o'clock news is hardly a source of pleasant dreams.

Yes, knowledge can bring us grief and sorrow. On the other hand, it also brings us awareness, compassion, and a sense of accountability. We are not alone in this world, and what we do here affects the lives of others on the opposite side of the earth.

Father, even when knowledge brings us sadness or anger, we can turn these unpleasant emotions into good with Your help and guidance. Show us what we need to do and how we can help repair the lives of others.

TAKING RESPONSIBILITY

Behold, the LORD's hand is
not shortened,
that it cannot save;
neither his ear heavy,
that it cannot hear.

ISAIAH 59:1 KJV

Being fallible, self-centered people, we usually look for ways to blame someone else when our lives go wrong. Ultimately, we are even tempted to wonder if something is wrong with God. Can't He hear our prayers? Is He too far away to pluck us from danger?

The answer, of course, is that God is still—and will forever be—the same. He doesn't change, He hears fine, and He has all the power He needs. The problem is with us, not Him. We do God a grave injustice when we try to shift the blame to Him instead of taking responsibility for our own lives.

Father, forgive us when we try to unburden our own shoulders and put the blame on You.

NOTHING BUT LOVE

And the Lord turned
and looked at Peter. . . .
So Peter went out and wept bitterly.

LUKE 22:61–62 NKJV

"And the Lord turned and looked at Peter." What did Peter see in that brief glance from his doomed Savior? Disappointment? Anger? Probably not, although both would have been justified.

No, Peter saw nothing but love in that glance, which is why he ran out and wept so bitterly. He had promised undying love, and then he had denied his Lord. Worse yet, the Lord still loved him, unworthy as he was.

The next time you and your spouse disagree, remember the Lord's reaction to disappointment. Stun your spouse with love.

Father, help us react to betrayal with love, following Jesus' example in our own lives.

1 + 1 = 1?

For this reason a man will leave
his father and mother
and be united to his wife,
and they will become one flesh.

GENESIS 2:24 NIV

The idea that one plus one equals one is hard for us to grasp, but that's what happens in marriage. A man and a woman come to the marriage ceremony as two separate individuals; when they walk back up the aisle, they are one couple. They both still maintain their individuality—nothing is taken away from either of them—yet now they are "Mr. and Mrs.," a new shared identity.

In a way, attending a wedding is similar to celebrating a birth, which is why the recessional of the new couple is often heartily applauded. Where once there were two, now there is one, and life goes on.

Father, help us both as we begin our new life as one. We have much to learn and experience in this new state of marriage but know You are there for us, celebrating with us.

"The Couple"

The body is a unit,
though it is made up of many parts;
and though its parts are many,
they form one body.

1 Corinthians 12:12 NIV

It's like the old story of the blind men and the elephant. The trunk isn't the elephant, or the ear, or the tail. Yet the elephant wouldn't be itself without each of its parts. Likewise, a new couple cannot be understood by looking at just the husband or the wife. They are only parts of something bigger than themselves.

Of course, without one of them there is no "couple" at all. Friends and families of a new couple will have to learn that they are now dealing with a new unit with new priorities. John may not be able to go to the game every weekend, and Mary may no longer call her parents twice a week, all because now they are "John and Mary."

Lord, help everyone affected by our marriage understand the changes we will be going through as a new couple. Right now we are so absorbed with each other that we may overlook the feelings of our friends and family. Give them patience and help them be happy for our happiness.

FINANCIAL WORKOUT

*Let no debt
remain outstanding.*

ROMANS 13:8 NIV

One of the first hurdles of any marriage is money. Before you married, you had your bills and he had his, and you dealt with them in your own ways. As a couple, you now have "our" debts, and "we" had better come to a fast agreement on how money should be handled. How you work it out is up to you, but work it out you must.

You now have joint debts, in addition to individual ones, twice as many Christmas presents to buy, money to be saved and invested for children and retirement, insurance policies, and even a joint income-tax form. If you are unable to come up with a workable financial plan, get help from someone you trust.

Father, give us guidance in straightening out our financial life as a couple. With Your help and some good advice from others, we can do this.

KEEP OUT!

Like one who
seizes a dog by the ears is
a passer-by who
meddles in a quarrel not his own.

PROVERBS 26:17 NIV

No one with any sense would walk up to a strange dog and grab it by the ears. You never know what the dog will do, but since its ears are very sensitive, an unpleasant scene is likely to result. Police officers hate domestic disturbance calls for the same reason: They can be dangerous to anyone who butts in.

You may think you're being helpful when you try to help someone else's marriage, but realize that both parties may turn on you.

Lord, teach us that while wanting to help others is an admirable trait, a certain amount of caution is necessary. If we're not careful, we will end up being hurt ourselves, especially if the matter is none of our business.

In His Timing

I know how to be abased,
and I know how to abound.
Everywhere and in all things I have learned
both to be full and to be hungry,
both to abound and to suffer need.
I can do all things through Christ
who strengthens me.

PHILIPPIANS 4:12–13 NKJV

We go through a lot of changes in our lives, some of which we try desperately to avoid, and all of which teach us something. Eating hot dogs and beans several times a week isn't fun, but we do learn that the most humble of diets can keep us alive. A long period of unemployment can take a house away from us, but we soon find we can survive in a tiny apartment, too.

No one wants to go through hard times. We'd rather learn to abound and be full, but if God is with us, we can do anything. Perhaps the most important thing we can learn from hard times is that God stays with us through them all and brings us out of them in His time.

Father, Your constant and faithful love will bring us through any trial we may have to face. When times are good again, we will not forget the strength You gave us in our darkest moments.

FORGIVE AND MOVE ON

Bearing with one another,
and forgiving one another,
if anyone has a complaint against another;
even as Christ forgave you,
so you also must do.

COLOSSIANS 3:13 NKJV

Have you noticed that it's easier to forgive a stranger than a spouse? Unlike your partner, you aren't emotionally invested in a stranger. But when a husband or wife hurts you, you really hurt. Part of the pain comes from knowing that your spouse is well aware of exactly what will hurt you and uses that knowledge with intent.

The Bible gives us no quarter here: "so you also must do." You must forgive each other and move on, for the sake of your witness and your marriage, no matter how betrayed you feel.

Lord, when we fight unfairly with each other and intentionally hurt each other, give us the strength we need to forgive, no matter how hard that is to do.

That Ever Changing Love

But above all. . . put on love,
which is the bond of perfection.

Colossians 3:14 nkjv

Why do over 50 percent of marriages end in divorce? More important, why do 50 percent of marriages endure for life? What do half of the people understand that the other half do not?

Maybe they understand the true nature of love. Love is always changing, never static. It grows and matures as we do. Love is giving, not taking, forgiving, not abandoning. As people change, so does the nature of their love, and passions flare and subside.

The wise person, however, understands change and even welcomes the variety it brings to life. No, your spouse will not be twenty-five forever, but what fifty-year-old would want to live with someone who lacks the depth and wisdom to understand him?

Lord, help us adjust to the changing nature of love and welcome its growth the same way we welcome the growth of a child.

SHARING GOOD FORTUNE

*"For the poor will never cease
from the land;
therefore I command you, saying,
'You shall open your hand wide
to your brother,
to your poor and your needy.' "*

DEUTERONOMY 15:11 NKJV

When you come down to it, the Bible is a pretty realistic book, portraying the harshness of life and showing us how to deal with it. There will always be poor people in the land, but we are to open our hands wide to them.

We are told to reach into our pockets, pull out what we have, and give whatever is needed, not dribble a few coins out of a clenched fist while hiding the big bills. This isn't a suggestion; it's a command, and a pretty firm one at that. How we obey that command could very well determine the fate of the world.

Father, help us put our wishes and desires aside when faced with the poor and share our good fortune without grumbling or regret.

I Love You

My little children,
let us not love in word or in tongue,
but in deed and in truth.

1 John 3:18 NKJV

It's easy to say, "I love you," especially when we want something from another. The words just fall off our tongues, never even going through our brains on the way. You can fool a lot of people into believing those words, too, at least until your actions prove otherwise.

Christians who have been brought up to love generously can be guilty of using those three words inappropriately, too. There are a lot of huggy-kissy Christians who would be well advised to keep their distance until others can see if their words are backed up by their lives.

Father, let us show our love to the world in practical, honest ways,
not in meaningless words that can be misunderstood or disbelieved.

Totally Faithful

For no matter how many
promises God has made,
they are "Yes" in Christ.
And so through him the "Amen" is
spoken by us to the glory of God.

2 Corinthians 1:20 niv

There are no *"nos"* in God's promises. He never denies something He has said He will do or fails to follow through on a pledge He has made. Totally faithful to the words He has spoken, He comes through in the darkest moment or on the sunniest of days.

Friends may deny you, your boss may fire you, and your spouse may fail you. They're human, after all. And no human has unlimited control over life.

But the "yes" God says in Jesus doesn't change. Not only will He stand by you in this life, in the next life He will bring you to eternal life. His eternal "yes" lasts a lifetime, and not just through the latest rough patch.

Have you said "amen" to Jesus, the great Amen? Do you know His truth today?

Lord, You alone are the final truth, the final yes that ends all nos.
Be the yes of our lives.

GRACE

So I made up my mind that
I would not make
another painful visit to you.

2 CORINTHIANS 2:1 NIV

S ome relationships are trouble from the start. You meet a person and just don't get on. If it's a casual acquaintance, you probably have a tacit agreement not to meet too often. It's better for you both that way.

But it's different when it's a family member, and especially difficult when it's someone in your spouse's family. If that person lives far away, you don't meet all that often and can work around it. But nearby relatives provide a greater challenge.

Perhaps you need to talk out an issue and come to an agreement. Make a try. But if that fails, don't feel you must spend a lot of time battling with a family member. That could ruin your witness for Christ.

Paul didn't force himself on the Corinthians after they had a painful visit. Neither did he give up on the church. Like Paul and the Corinthian church, place a little distance between you temporarily, spend time in prayer and thought, and things may gain a new perspective.

Even as Christians, we don't always agree with family. Give us grace for those difficult relationships.

REACHING OUT

*"I will sweep away everything
from the face of the earth,"
declares the LORD.*

ZEPHANIAH 1:2 NIV

A day is coming when God will set the world right. Instead of saving humanity in an ark, He will pronounce an ultimate judgment.

Most of us would like to see sin wiped out and righteousness rule. We'd like our enemies to realize they are wrong without suffering much. Still, the graphic imagery of Zephaniah's book seems unnecessarily unpleasant.

But God takes sin seriously. His goal is to eradicate all sin, something that can't be done with sweet phrases. God ruthlessly sweeps sin out of His people's lives and out of the world. Anything less would deny the immense price His Son paid on the cross to connect sinful people with Himself.

Sin isn't pleasant, and God never calls it that. But He's also not silent about its impact or ultimate end. He warned you to avoid an awful judgment. Have you listened? Have you shared that news with others?

*Lord, we don't relish Your judgment, though we know it is just.
Help us to reach out to those who need to know You.*

GOD'S POWER

To him who is able
to keep you from falling
and to present you before
his glorious presence without fault
and with great joy. . .

JUDE 24 NIV

Trying to obey God can be hard work. You have the best intentions but things keep going wrong. Even doing what is right doesn't seem to solve the problem. You're stuck.

Maybe you've started to rely on your own power. Getting caught up in dotting the i's and crossing the t's of faith traps you in legalism. Doing right isn't a matter of earning something with God but showing how much you love Him. Love needs to flow from appreciation, not obligation.

Oddly, you can't please God without God's power doing that work in your life. Try to please God on your own and you fail.

Jesus alone makes you perfect and presents you to the Father in a spotless white robe, pure and undefiled. You can't put on that robe under your own power or enter God's glorious throne room without Him. Share that joy with Him by letting Him work in you.

Lord, we want to appreciate You, not feel obligated. Work in our lives today.

His Will, His Way

*He hath inclosed my ways
with hewn stone,
he hath made my paths crooked.*

LAMENTATIONS 3:9 KJV

When afflictions surround us, our path seems cut into stone. We can't seem to change direction, and we always seem to take the longest path to anywhere. We're blocked in by circumstances. We're no longer on a highway but a crooked little trail that seems to go nowhere.

Like the prophet, we feel frustration. *Why does God have us here?* we may wonder. It just doesn't seem to make sense.

Not all of God's ways are highways. Sometimes, to fulfill His will, He has to bring you down a side path of trouble. But in the end, by following His way, you'll be able to glorify God. He has not forgotten you. "His compassions fail not," testifies the prophet (v. 22). Hope lies just around the corner when you serve God.

Even the narrowest path leads to Him when you follow His will.

Lord, we know Your compassion hasn't failed us, even when the road is long and narrow. Thank You for leading us in Your way, even when it's a hard path.

PROSPER TODAY

Is not my word
like as a fire? saith the LORD;
and like a hammer that
breaketh the rock in pieces?

God's Word—whether written in the Bible or spoken—is powerful. To misrepresent it is to misrepresent His will and way. Those who do so may seem prosperous for a time, but God does not take their misdeeds lightly. One day they will be destroyed as if a hammer had pounded them in pieces.

When we speak about God's Word to each other, do we treat it respectfully or try to make it say whatever we want to hear? If we don't treat it with reverence, looking to see what God really has to say to us, we are like the false prophets Jeremiah dealt with. God is against such people and will see that they don't prosper.

Prosper today by listening carefully to God's Word and acting it out in your lives. Then the flame of His love will burn in your hearts and not destroy you.

Lord, let Your Spirit burn brightly in our hearts as we revere You and seek Your will through Your Word.

God's Provision

" 'The silver is mine
and the gold is mine,'
declares the LORD Almighty."

HAGGAI 2:8 NIV

You've planned a ministry together or in your church, but the money just doesn't seem to be in the budget. Should you or your church go into debt to make it happen?

One way God weeds out those ministries that are not His is to let them languish financially. People who get involved in otherwise godly things to make themselves look good will often run into financial troubles that end up wrecking their ministries.

That doesn't mean that every accounting problem is a sign that you're out of God's will. Sometimes it's just a test to make sure you're keeping your eyes on God and not seeking your own fame or the appreciation of others.

God owns all the money in the world. He will provide for that ministry He has in mind. Just tune in to Him and be clear that you're doing His will. He will provide a way.

Lord, we want to serve You, not gain kudos for ourselves. Whether it's a formal ministry or just the witness of our lives, let our actions glorify You.

FORGIVENESS AND HEALING

Return to the LORD your God,
for he is gracious and compassionate,
slow to anger and abounding in love,
and he relents from sending calamity.

JOEL 2:13 NIV

When God's people turn from Him, He does not immediately explode in anger. First, He calls them to repent and enjoy the relationship He's always wanted to share with them. Over the course of history, those who believe in Him have sometimes obeyed, and sometimes they have not.

If you've been married more than a short while, chances are you know how God feels. You want a close relationship with your spouse. You'd like to keep that honeymoon feeling forever. But it doesn't work that way. Sin always works into a marriage after time. Perhaps it's that irritating habit you never mentioned while you were dating or a lack of consideration that never occurred before marriage.

Seek forgiveness and healing together, instead of indulging in anger and calamities, and your relationship can deepen. You can't live on honeymoon love forever, but you can keep calamities at bay.

Lord, help us to seek forgiveness, not anger, as our first reaction. We want healing, not calamity, in our love.

TRUTH LIVES IN YOU

Because of the truth,
which lives in us
and will be with us forever.

2 JOHN 2 NIV

Try getting away from the truth, as a Christian, and you'll find it's still with you. Why? Because truth lives in you through Jesus, not just today but forever. You can't evade truth, and why should you? Being close to Jesus and knowing how He wants you to live gives you a wonderful life.

Living with lies messes up life, as even those of us who slip into untruths occasionally can testify. We may lie to gain some benefits and discover they're short-lived, if they come at all.

The results of lying aren't what we think they will be. We expect less trouble by evading truth but end up in more. If we make lying a life habit, we may seem to win in the short run, but we'll gain bad reputations and see many disasters in our lives.

God does repay lying—with trouble and spiritual death. If that's a harvest you don't want, don't do it!

Lord, You are truth. Keep living in us.

Draw Closer with Truth

Wherefore putting away lying,
speak every man truth
with his neighbour:
for we are members
one of another.

Ephesians 4:25 KJV

Do you tell the truth to your spouse? You should. After all, isn't he or she your closest neighbor? You truly are members one of another, even more closely connected to each other than to Christian brothers and sisters.

Living with a person who doesn't tell the truth is extremely aggravating. How do you know what to believe, when that person sometimes says what is so and sometimes doesn't? Instead of drawing closer, a couple will be divided by lies. Anger is likely to be their constant companion because one will hate being lied to and the other won't understand what the problem is.

If you want to be members of one another, you can't live with constant lies. Truth draws you closer as you trust each other. So put away those lies from your home as well as your church life.

Lord, we want to speak the truth to each other. Help us to put away those lies and trust each other.

SLOW TO ANGER

*The LORD is slow to anger
and great in power,
and will not at all
acquit the wicked.*

NAHUM 1:3 NKJV

Some people treat anger as a weapon. To manipulate others to their ways, they attack with sharp words or even physical violence.

Such reactions do not show a person's power but his weakness. A truly powerful person follows God in being slow to anger. But that does not mean a wrongdoer always gets away with evil. It just means rushed reactions are not a good thing.

As humans, we usually want quick results: judgment for the evildoer, at any cost. God promises to bring justice to every situation—but not on our time schedule or in our way.

We can trust in the God who is slow to anger because we have experienced His mercy. When we err or even sin intentionally, He is also slow to retaliate so that we can have time to come to Him in repentance.

Aren't we all glad swift justice is not always His?

Thank You, Lord, for being slow to anger. Teach us also to consider well before we open our mouths in judgment.

OUR REFUGE

*The L*ORD* is good,*
a stronghold in the day of trouble;
and He knows those who
trust in Him.

NAHUM 1:7 NKJV

W hen trouble comes, do you look to your checkbook, job security, or your spouse for protection?

We all hope those things remain solid, but the truth is that at some time, each can fail us. Money may not last, a job may disappear, and our spouses make mistakes. We can't always lean on them because they are earthly. The things that affect us affect them, too.

We need a refuge greater than the world, one that can stand up to it. As long as we look to earth for security, it evades us. Our stronghold, Nahum reminds us, can only be God. We can trust His goodness that even when He rains down judgment on those around us, He will not forget His children. We remain safe in His citadel when the world around us comes breaking apart.

Run to those arms. Enter the gates of the stronghold where you are known and protected. No enemy harms you there.

Thank You, Lord God, for being our protection. Keep us fast through all our trials.

FULLNESS

Israel is an empty vine,
he bringeth forth fruit unto himself:
according to the multitude of
his fruit he hath increased the altars;
according to the goodness of his land
they have made goodly images.

HOSEA 10:1 KJV

Emptiness fills those who turn away from God. They may crowd churches, but worshiping their own goodness and insisting on barren theologies leaves them empty, no matter how packed the sanctuary.

When we bring forth our own fruit, designed by us instead of God, we worship at altars that are not His. Many hurting people have run to spiritually empty congregations and thought they'd heard from God. No wonder these folks deny His power. False images have led them to ascribe to God something that has nothing to do with Him.

God's fruit isn't empty, though. When we worship at His altar, our theology isn't barren. God brings fullness to His people's lives when we set aside images of other gods and seek to serve Him alone.

Are you wholeheartedly serving Him today?

Lord, turn us from empty altars and toward true worship of You.

Send Us

Then I heard the voice of the Lord saying,
"Whom shall I send?
And who will go for us?"
And I said, "Here am I. Send me!"

ISAIAH 6:8 NIV

"The Bohemian disease" was what he was accused of having, but Martin Luther wasn't sick. In fact, he was one of the most spiritually well men in all of Europe.

His "disease" was that he agreed with the ideas of the fourteenth-century priest Jan Hus, a Bohemian who had pushed for church reform. John Wycliffe, the English Bible translator, had influenced Hus, and all three men seriously studied the Scriptures. Where the Bible and church practice didn't agree, they confronted a reluctant church.

The Reformation that sprang out of Luther's Ninety-five Theses, posted in 1517, was not the work of one man. A long line of churchmen had faithfully studied Scripture and responded to its commands. For many, saying "Here am I; send me" to God had resulted in excommunication and even death.

When you read Scripture, can you say, "Send us"? You could be part of that line of faithful servants.

Lord, we want to serve You with whole hearts, no matter what it costs.

UNIQUE PEOPLE

And Moses answered and said,
But, behold, they will not believe me,
nor hearken unto my voice:
for they will say,
The LORD hath not appeared unto thee.

EXODUS 4:1 KJV

If you have teenage children, you will often feel like Moses. At the precise time of life they most need your guidance and advice, they stop listening.

They no longer have the unquestioning faith in you that they had at age five. This is the time for them to question anyone in authority, especially their parents. As aggravating as it can be, teenagers need to think things through for themselves, to build their own values and claim their own territory as individuals. They need to say, "This is what I believe."

They won't emerge from this period as carbon copies of you. And who would want them to be? They emerge as themselves, the unique people they want to be for the rest of their lives.

Father, during these emotional and trying years, please be there for our children. Guide them as they explore their own identities, and give us confidence that they will turn out to be the wonderful people they have the power to be, with Your help.

GOD OF LOVE

For when they shall rise from the dead,
they neither marry,
nor are given in marriage;
but are as the angels
which are in heaven.

MARK 12:25 KJV

If we have a good marriage, we find it is difficult to accept this verse. Sure, we want to be like the angels, but it's nearly impossible to think of eternity without our spouses. Will we at least remember each other and the life we've had together? Will we still love each other?

Our problem is that we know so little about eternity and even less about angels. We are emotionally tied to what we know and afraid to give up what we have, even though God promises we will be happy. All we can know for sure is that God is a God of love.

Father, we know that You have only the best in mind for our future and that being with You will be more wonderful than we can possibly imagine. Calm our fears and lead us to trust Your plan.

CONSISTENCY

That ye all speak the same thing,
and that there be no divisions among you;
but that ye be perfectly joined together
in the same mind and
in the same judgment.

1 CORINTHIANS 1:10 KJV

D o your children play you and your spouse off each other to get what they want? If Dad gives the "wrong" answer, they go talk to Mom, hoping for a better result. You have to learn to outflank them, to refuse to make the decision before the two of you talk about it, especially if it's an important one. Sometimes a conversation isn't needed, and you can give your answer after just looking at your spouse. Sometimes you will disagree and have to work out a mutually acceptable compromise. At other times you will give a quick answer on your own, knowing what your spouse will say. The trick is not to let your children divide you, to be "in the same mind and in the same judgment."

Lord, our children need consistency, and we need to support each other in our decisions. Help us to be of one mind, for the sake of our children.

Moving On

Then said the LORD,
Doest thou well to be angry?

JONAH 4:4 KJV

J onah had predicted disaster, but God acted with mercy, contradicted Jonah's prophecy, and left him looking like a fool. Jonah was ticked off, to put it mildly. Then God asked if it was a good idea to be angry, given the situation.

People make fools of us all the time, changing their minds, contradicting our decisions, doing whatever they want in spite of our good advice. Our feelings are hurt and our reputations may even be damaged, but what good does it do to be angry? The decision has been taken out of our hands, and all we can do is move on.

Lord, when someone makes us look foolish, help us control our unproductive anger, knowing that You have everything under control and things will all work out the way they were meant to work out.

THREE, NOT TWO

The LORD hath been
witness between thee
and the wife of thy youth,
against whom thou hast dealt treacherously:
yet is she thy companion,
and the wife of thy covenant.

MALACHI 2:14 KJV

Perhaps things haven't been going very well in your marriage recently. You haven't "dealt treacherously" with each other, but you haven't felt particularly loving either. Such "cool" phases happen in the best of marriages.

Now is a good time to remember that a marriage concerns three people, not two, and that the Lord gave you your spouse and knows exactly how you feel. He wants your marriage to thrive. Give Him time to help you. Don't toss away a gift of God.

Lord, when things go sour in our relationship, give us the patience and determination we need to hang in there and work things out between us with Your help.

CHILDREN TO ADULTS

I have no greater joy than
to hear that my children
walk in truth.

3 JOHN 4 KJV

Somewhere along the line it will dawn on you that your children are now adults and it's time to "butt out." They aren't perfect yet, but neither are you. You did the best you could for them and have much to be proud of. They are not only functioning adults, but they also turned out to be talented, compassionate, faithful, and whatever other good qualities you see in them.

If they would let you, you would be proud to be their friend. This is your reward for all those hard years of work and worry. If they still need to improve here and there, you've got a few years left to work on them.

Father, thank You for helping our children grow into competent adults who no longer need or want our daily supervision. We're proud of them all and never could have gotten this far without Your help.

PROCRASTINATION

Go thy way for this time;
when I have a convenient season,
I will call for thee.

ACTS 24:25 KJV

Felix didn't want to hear any more from Paul. What he had heard of the gospel upset him, so he put off making any decision until a more "convenient" time.

Procrastination is always the easiest way out. We do it all the time. "Shouldn't we volunteer to teach Sunday school?" "Let's wait and see if they really need us." "Did you talk to Junior about drugs?" "He's too young. Next year."

Sometimes we do need more time to make important decisions, and at other times we just put off important actions out of fear or distaste. The trick is in knowing when you really need to think something through and when you're just copping out.

Lord, help us make decisions when they need to be made, not put them off until a more "convenient" time.

OVERCOME EVIL WITH GOOD

Therefore
if thine enemy hunger,
feed him;
if he thirst, give him drink. . . .
Be not overcome of evil,
but overcome evil with good.

ROMANS 12:20–21 KJV

I t's so easy to be overcome by evil. When someone treats us poorly, we either fight or flee. It's a natural reaction to strike back or just get away before any more damage can be done.

But we have a third choice that we rarely even consider: We can overcome evil with good. We can stand our ground, smile politely, and treat our enemies with love and consideration. If we keep it up, they'll either leave us alone or begin to change their minds about us.

Let's give them something more worthwhile to think about.

Father, when someone strikes out at us, give us the strength to answer hatred with love and aggression with peace.

WISHES AND DREAMS

Neither shalt thou desire
thy neighbour's wife,
neither shalt thou covet
thy neighbour's house, his field,
or his manservant, or his maidservant,
his ox, or his ass, or any thing
that is thy neighbour's.

DEUTERONOMY 5:21 KJV

To covet means to feel unreasonable desire for something that belongs to another. It's more than just wishing for a new car when your neighbor drives one home. You want that car, the one your neighbor has, not one just like it. And you want it badly. You can see how this can cause a lot of problems, especially if you covet your neighbor's wife!

The Lord knows we all have wishes and dreams, but He wants us to have the right perspective on them and not let them control our lives or make us act irrationally. Wish for anything you want; covet nothing.

Lord, help us keep our desires and dreams under control, knowing You will provide for us and give us the joy of answered prayers.

In Secret

But when you give to the needy,
do not let your left hand know
what your right hand is doing,
so that your giving may be in secret.
Then your Father,
who sees what is done in secret,
will reward you.

MATTHEW 6:3–4 NIV

We all know generous souls who require only one reward for their charity: recognition. Some are satisfied with a simple thank-you, while others want their names on a building or a mention of their gift from the pulpit. They're really not asking for much, and we can understand how they feel, but they are seeking a limited human reward.

God promises them much more if they keep their gifts a secret. The next time you give of your resources, try doing so in secret and see how much more rewarding your gift will feel to you.

Father, we know Your rewards are far greater than anything we could receive from others. Help us seek to please You with our gifts, not our friends and neighbors.

NEEDED CORRECTION

For men are not
cast off by the Lord forever.
Though he brings grief,
he will show compassion,
so great is his unfailing love.
For he does not willingly bring affliction
or grief to the children of men.

LAMENTATIONS 3:31–33 NIV

God doesn't like punishing us any more than we enjoy punishing our children. The truth is, sometimes we need correction.

When was the last time you had to punish your children? You tried everything else you could think of first, but nothing worked. You couldn't get their attention any other way, and, as trite as it sounds, it did hurt you more than it hurt them.

The next time you feel that God might be punishing you, take time to figure out why. Have there been inner warnings you ignored? Confess your sins and know they will be forgiven.

Father, You may correct us when we stray from Your way, but Your love is never ending, and You will never punish us unfairly.

WISDOM

*When the queen of Sheba
heard of Solomon's fame,
she came to Jerusalem to
test him with hard questions.*

2 CHRONICLES 9:1 NIV

The queen of Sheba was much like today's woman. She had heard wonderful things about a man—someone probably even told her he had a great personality! —but she had her own questions. He was rich and powerful, but so were a lot of bums, then and now. He had to prove himself to her before she would believe half the things others said.

Women do the same thing today, ignoring the outer trappings of a man and asking the hard questions that determine the fate of a relationship. Solomon passed the test, as you did if you are married. Give thanks to the Lord for the wisdom He has given you and the love that wisdom brought you.

Father, thank You for helping us find each other and giving us the wisdom we needed to pass the tests of courtship.

Our Father

"I will be a Father to you,
and you will be
my sons and daughters,
says the Lord Almighty."

2 Corinthians 6:18 niv

S ooner or later, we all become orphans. It's devastating to wake up one morning knowing our parents are not just a telephone call away, and knowing, too, that they will never see any future grandchildren. We feel so lonely. We're never ready to stop being someone's beloved child. Other members of the older generation, aunts and uncles, can ease some of our pain, but soon they will be gone, too.

If you are facing times like these, accept God's offer to be your Father. Bring your problems to Him, listen for His advice, and know you are still loved.

Father, help us through these difficult times of being suddenly alone in the world. Pour Your love upon us as we turn to You in our grief.

Been There, Done That

*"Ask the former generations
and find out what
their fathers learned,
for we were born only yesterday
and know nothing."*

Job 8:8–9 NIV

Reinventing the wheel is a terrible waste of time, and living without understanding the past only dooms us to future mistakes that could be avoided. Why go around and around in the same circle when your elders have already done that lap and can show you a shortcut?

Today information is readily available on almost any subject—more information than we can ever process ourselves. We need to know what information is useful and profitable and what is just junk. Ask those who have already been there, done that.

Father, our individual lives are short, but collectively we have ages of wisdom and history to help us. Give us the grace to listen to our elders and help humanity move forward, with Your guidance.

DISCERNING TRUTH

Beloved,
do not believe every spirit,
but test the spirits,
whether they are of God;
because many false prophets
have gone out into the world.
By this you know the Spirit of God:
Every spirit that confesses that Jesus Christ
has come in the flesh is of God.

1 JOHN 4:1–2 NKJV

With a worldwide increase of interest in spirituality of all types, Christians need to keep on their toes to discern the truth. Some proponents of these spiritual movements sound logical and good, so how can you tell a false prophet from a real one? Granted, a false prophet is unmasked by his errors, but it could be years before he's proven wrong. What do you do in the meantime?

The best way to avoid becoming enmeshed in heresy is to ask one simple question: Does the person, movement, or philosophy espouse Jesus as the Savior? If not, back off and have nothing to do with such thinking.

Father, give us the ability to discern the truth when we hear it and avoid following anyone who does not come in the name of Your Son.

KEEPING BALANCE

Give me neither poverty nor riches—
Feed me with the food allotted to me;
lest I be full and deny You, and say,
"Who is the Lord?"
Or lest I be poor and steal,
and profane the name of my God.

PROVERBS 30:8–9 NKJV

There is always danger in extremes. If we're rich, we tend to take the credit for our own success and not give it to God to whom it belongs. If we're poor, we may sin in desperation and dishonor the God we claim to follow. Neither extreme is a good witness to others.

Fortunately, most of us are somewhere between the two extremes of wealth and poverty, neither denying God's work in our lives nor profaning His name through our actions. It's a thin line we walk, but God will help us keep our balance.

Father, we thank You for all the blessings You have given us, whether they are many or few. May we live our lives in such a way that others will see You in our lives and believe.

PEACE WITH BROTHERS AND SISTERS

Therefore if thou
bring thy gift to the altar,
and there rememberest that thy brother
hath ought against thee;
leave there thy gift before the altar,
and go thy way;
first be reconciled to thy brother,
and then come and offer thy gift.

MATTHEW 5:23–24 KJV

It's easy to offer our gifts to the Father. It makes us feel good to be at peace with Him and contribute our time and money to the work of the church. But Jesus reminds us that in order to be at peace with Him, we first need to be at peace with our brothers and sisters. This is not a simple matter.

Who is your brother, and how have you wronged him? The wider you define the word "brother," the more impossible the job becomes. Surely you can't be expected to resolve centuries of slavery, oppression, and wrongdoing on your own—can you? Seek God's guidance on this confusing matter and follow His leading.

Father, show us where we have wronged others and what we can do to be reconciled with them, then give us the courage to do Your will in this world.

GIVE IT TO GOD

Take therefore
no thought for the morrow:
for the morrow shall take
thought for the things of itself.
Sufficient unto the day is the evil thereof.

MATTHEW 6:34 KJV

Most of us are born worriers. Some things we can handle fairly well, while others keep us awake all night. If things are going fairly well one day, we still lie awake waiting for the second shoe to drop, knowing it will drop, wondering if we will survive the fall.

This is exactly what Jesus warns against: anticipatory worrying. Life provides us with plenty to deal with in one day, so why look ahead to tomorrow's problems? God knows exactly what we need and will provide it when we need it. That should leave us all with a little extra time to "seek ye first the kingdom of God, and his righteousness" (Matthew 6:33 KJV).

Father, we trust You for the basics of life but continue to worry about them, as if our worrying could do us any good. Strengthen our faith in Your provision so we can concentrate on the work You have in mind for us to accomplish.

Good Stewardship

House and riches are
the inheritance of fathers:
and a prudent wife is
from the LORD.

PROVERBS 19:14 KJV

If you have ever come into some unexpected money, especially inherited money, you know how fast it can disappear without careful stewardship. A new home, a couple of cars, a visit from the IRS, and you're right back where you started. All those years of saving and going without wiped out in less than one generation!

On the other hand, money we make and save on our own, through prudent living and attention to details, we rarely waste. If you and your spouse are carefully saving for the future, you know why the writer of this psalm says a prudent wife is a gift from the Lord.

Father, we'll never be rich, but we can be careful stewards of our financial resources, with Your help.

PRIORITIES

Prepare thy work without,
and make it fit for thyself in the field;
and afterwards build thine house.

PROVERBS 24:27 KJV

Do you remember seeing old photos of early western plains settlers, all lined up in front of a sod house with their children, horse, and dog? The floor of the house was nothing but dirt, and the walls and roof were sod. There were no windows; the inside of the house was filled with smoke. It was shelter, that's all. Until the ground was broken and the first crop planted, no one wasted time building a real house, because without a crop they would all die.

We still need to prioritize today: first a job, then a lot of saving, then the house. Any time you see your desires rushing ahead of your means, think of those pioneers and cut up your credit cards.

Father, set our priorities in order for us, and give us the patience we need to realize our dreams one step at a time.

Resting in Him

My soul finds rest in
God alone;
my salvation comes from him.

Psalm 62:1 NIV

I f our to-do list is longer than the days we have to accomplish things, we're too busy. Holidays can pull us into too many parties, special church occasions, and so on. Although all those things may be good, when they mount up and we become spiritually bedraggled by them, we've lost our balance in life.

True rest isn't attained in family parties, church meetings, or even good works. None of those offer the peace we're looking for. We can find true peace when we spend time with God. That may be in a special service, but we also need time together with Him in prayer and His Word. If we're attempting to do God's will without tapping directly into Him, we're out of His will, however busy we are.

We need to spend time today resting in Him alone.

Thank You, Lord, for being our rest. When life gets too hectic, remind us that we need to stop what we're doing and rest in You.

INTIMATE LOVE

I am my beloved's,
and my beloved is mine.

SONG OF SOLOMON 6:3 NKJV

Within marriage we feel such mutual interconnectedness that over time we as partners become difficult to separate. Think of one member of a couple that's been married for years, and it may be hard not to remember the other, too. When two people who live together in marriage have the same goals, attitudes, and aims, we naturally connect them.

But this verse isn't only talking about the interconnectedness of two human lovers. The Song of Solomon describes God's bride, the Church, as she shares love with Him.

As Christians, you are part of His Church—God's beloved. You are His, and He is yours. Just as you closely identify with your spouse, God identifies with you. He connects closely with those whom He loves.

Two who share both human love and God's love have the best of this world and the next. Draw close to Him today.

Lord, thank You for such intimate love. Draw us closer to You.

THROUGH THE AGES

Ram begot Amminadab,
Amminadab begot Nahshon,
and Nahshon begot Salmon.

MATTHEW 1:4 NKJV

R un a computer spell check on Amminadab or Nahshon and you probably won't get any spelling options. Your machine can't recognize these as names of people who lived and made up part of Christ's earthly lineage, unless you add their names to your software's dictionary.

Unlike a computer, God recognizes people through the ages: the forgotten folk who did extraordinary works for Him, and those who struggled to do His will. People, perhaps, just like you.

A computer may not recognize your name, either, but God knows you, your day-to-day issues, and the works you do for Him. He joined you and your spouse together in marriage and knows each of you intimately. Every detail of your lives is open to Him, and He meets needs no computer could begin to touch.

You are loved deeply and satisfyingly by God. He's never forgotten you, and He never will.

Lord, thank You for remembering us, even when the world forgets.

OBEDIENCE

After His mother Mary was
betrothed to Joseph,
before they came together,
she was found with child
of the Holy Spirit.

MATTHEW 1:18 NKJV

Scripture doesn't tell us what words Mary used to explain this unusual event to Joseph. Although Luke describes her joyful acceptance of the news that she would bear God's Son, nowhere are we told of this most intimate conversation.

Surely Mary must have been nervous. After all, Joseph knew he wasn't the father. How would he react? Though she knew her betrothed was a godly man and that God would help her, she must have felt a moment of nervousness. Could this ruin her relationship with her promised husband? Mary gave God wholehearted obedience anyway, trusting that bearing the Messiah would still be a blessing.

We've faced similar worrisome choices: *Will doing right be good for our marriage? Will God be there for us?*

If we follow Mary's example of implicit obedience, God comes through. Like her we can trust that He who calls us to obey also holds the future in His hands.

Lord, we want to obey You, no matter the cost. Give us courage to do Your will.

WILLINGNESS TO DO RIGHT

Then Joseph,
being aroused from sleep,
did as the angel of the Lord
commanded him and took to him his wife.

MATTHEW 1:24 NKJV

What a kind, honest, God-fearing man was Joseph! Faced with the news that Mary was pregnant, he still loved her enough not to want to shame her. Knowing her baby wasn't his child, he wanted to do what was right before God. As her promised husband, he decided to follow the Law and divorce her, but quietly.

How surprised he must have been when an angel visited him and told him to take Mary as his wife. Unhesitatingly, he obeyed, perhaps secretly joyous that Mary had not betrayed him.

Like Joseph, are you facing troubles? Do you still treat your spouse with kindness and gentleness? Or have you started an anger-kindling spat? Are trials your time to show your stuff or take it out on your spouse?

God blessed Joseph for his willingness to do what was right and the godly way he responded to trouble. Will He do any less for you?

Lord, when we face troubles, help us to respond in a way that honors You.

Unexpected Blessings

Also the neighbor women
gave him a name,
saying, "There is a son born to Naomi."
And they called his name Obed.
He is the father of Jesse,
the father of David.

RUTH 4:17 NKJV

God's Word is full of unexpected blessings. Naomi, a woman whose life had become bitter because she'd lost her entire family, received the blessing of a grandson.

But Naomi's not the only blessed one. For Obed becomes part of the lineage of Jesus, the promised and long-expected Savior of all mankind. Out of Naomi's temporary sorrow came a blessing for the world. After all, if Naomi's daughter-in-law Ruth had never married her second husband, Obed could never have been born.

Are you and your spouse feeling very "unblessed" today? Perhaps that unexpected blessing from God is just around the corner. When it comes, His blessing may impact more than you and your family alone. People will call you blessed if you remain faithful to Him in your trials.

Lord Jesus, we know Your blessings are at work in our lives. Keep us faithful when we can't see them.

A STABLE

" 'But you, Bethlehem,
in the land of Judah,
are by no means least among
the rulers of Judah;
for out of you will come a ruler
who will be the shepherd
of my people Israel.' "

MATTHEW 2:6 NIV

J esus doesn't look to enter only the world's important places. He wasn't born in Jerusalem, Israel's largest city, near important people. He came simply and quietly to the small place of God's promise, to Bethlehem.

He still doesn't pick the most exciting or important places or people. Jesus slips into hard hearts and into cold, dank places that have opened just a crack to Him, and creates of them a temple.

You may not describe your heart as a Jerusalem for God, but He's not asking for worldly greatness. Jerusalem, Israel's largest city, was not where Jesus was born but where He died an agonizing death.

He's looking for a stable that will receive Him, not a palace. Are you willing to become a temple in Bethlehem?

Father God, thank You for sending Your Son into our hard hearts.
Make them places where You are worshiped.

PRAISE FOR TOMORROW

"And you, child,
will be called the prophet
of the Highest;
for you will go before
the face of the Lord
to prepare His ways."

LUKE 1:76 NKJV

This is the same man speaking who asked an angel, "How shall I know this?" (v. 18). Zacharias's doubt turned to a glorious faith that shone in his prophecy about his son, John. Now that Zacharias saw God's "results," his faith burned strong. God could speak through him in a clear promise. But unbelief had silenced him for months.

If God were to prevent us from speaking when we lost faith, would we go months—or even years—in silence? By doubting His promises in Scripture or the still, small voice that leads us in His path, will we go down in Christian history as a pair of Zachariases?

God doesn't call us to believe when the child is born, but when it's conceived. He promises He'll bring something to pass, and we need to trust in Him for nine months.

But we don't need to wait that long to shout His praises.

Lord, we want to praise You today for Your plans for tomorrow. Help us trust in You before we see every outcome.

PRAISE AND WORSHIP

And, lo, the angel of the Lord
came upon them, and the glory of the Lord
shone round about them:
and they were sore afraid.

LUKE 2:9 KJV

Fear of God? That concept is foreign to many of us. We see God as our best buddy, as someone who would never hurt us. Painful things, some try to believe, never come from God.

True, God does not cause needless pain. He loves us deeply. Yet we often forget that pain often precedes growth, and a sinful human, confronted by pure holiness, is likely to feel the pain of inadequacy. One who has done wrong wants to run from Him who has never erred, even if He doesn't directly confront that sin.

Faced with the angel of the Lord, the shepherds quaked. They knew they could never measure up to God. If He held their sins against them, they had no recourse. After confronting them with His glory, God sent a small, helpless baby whom the shepherds could worship without fear. They could understand Him without running away.

Are you worshiping the Child—or are you on the run?

Lord God, we don't want to run from You. We praise You for being our salvation.

IN CHARGE

And it came to pass
in those days that a decree
went out from Caesar Augustus
that all the world
should be registered.

LUKE 2:1 NKJV

When Caesar Augustus, one of Rome's greatest emperors, decreed that a census should be taken, all the empire moved to do his bidding.

As he made this decision, the Roman ruler was not thinking of obeying a God he didn't believe in. He had no knowledge of a promise made to a virgin or prophecies written in ancient texts. Yet his "independent" move brought to pass God's will.

When God is in charge, He brings amazing things to pass. People who don't even believe in Him may cause His will to happen for Christians. Seemingly impossible situations suddenly change. A knotty problem disappears.

When our lives are out of control, it's time to put them in the control of One who rules all, even the hearts of unbelieving emperors.

Lord, thank You for controlling our lives. Work Your will in them today.

LIFE'S INTERRUPTIONS

He went there to
register with Mary,
who was pledged to
be married to him
and was expecting a child.

LUKE 2:5 NIV

Joseph and Mary were obeying God when, at a time when any woman would be wise not to travel far, they packed up and visited Bethlehem.

How easy it might have been for the couple to complain—wasn't this babe the most important one in the world? *Lord, it isn't safe for a woman close to the end of her pregnancy to travel so far,* Mary might have objected. Instead, they did what was put before them without complaint.

That simple obedience had a powerful result. Through that move, God fulfilled Micah 5:2, that Israel's ruler would be born in Bethlehem, not Nazareth.

When "life" seems to interrupt your plans, do you complain or adapt? Can you see it as part of God's plan and not just an irritant? God might use that interruption to create a great moment in your life.

Lord, use every interruption in our lives to Your glory.

WISE MEN

Now after Jesus
was born in Bethlehem. . .
in the days of Herod the king. . .
wise men from the East came
to Jerusalem, saying,
"Where is He who has been born
King of the Jews?"

MATTHEW 2:1–2 NKJV

For wise men, these don't seem very astute. Walking into a king's palace and asking about another king seems to be looking for trouble.

The men from the East may have had some wisdom, but they couldn't read minds. They obviously didn't know the full situation, and they didn't know a thing about wicked King Herod.

Even the wisest human beings cannot know everything. Extremely discerning folks still make mistakes because they don't have enough information.

The only wisdom that never fails is from God, and because the wise men's hearts were right and they were obeying Him, He guided them away from danger and kept His Son safe.

Like those men, we don't have to rely on our own abilities. We can seek wisdom far greater than ours in God. Have you done that together today?

Lord, give us Your wisdom. On our own, we will only fail.

FAITHFUL TO EVERY PROMISE

"Sovereign Lord,
as you have promised,
you now dismiss your servant in peace.
For my eyes have seen
your salvation."

LUKE 2:29–30 NIV

God keeps His promises: the ones He makes to us personally and the ones He's made to the world and spoken through Scripture.

In this passage, the Father had just shown His faithfulness by fulfilling a centuries-old promise that He made to the Jews as soon as Adam fell. A Savior would redeem them. But He also fulfilled a personal promise to a man named Simeon whom the Holy Spirit had promised would see the infant Savior.

Are you confident God will keep His promises? When God makes them, it's not just in the abstract. He means His promises for people—all of us who believe in Him.

If you can trust that He gave us His Son, you can trust Him when He moves you to change jobs, take on a spiritual risk, or give unselfishly. He hasn't broken a promise yet, and He won't start with you.

Thank You, God, for Your faithfulness to every promise. We can trust in You.